God, Sex and Love

GOD, SEX & LOVE

An Exercise in Ecumenical Ethics

JACK DOMINIAN
AND
HUGH MONTEFIORE

SCM PRESS
London

TRINITY PRESS INTERNATIONAL
Philadelphia

First published 1989

SCM Press
26–30 Tottenham Road
London N1 4BZ

Trinity Press International
3725 Chestnut Street
Philadelphia, Pa. 19104

Copyright © Jack Dominian (Preface and chapters 2 and 3) and
Hugh Montefiore (chapters 1, 4 and 5) 1989.

Library of Congress Cataloging-in-Publication Data

Dominian. Jack 1929–
    God, sex, and love: an exercise in ecumenical ethics/Jack
Dominian and Hugh Montefiore.
    p.   cm.
    Includes bibliographical references.
    ISBN 0–334–00533–7
    1. Sex—Religious aspects—Christianity.   2. Sexual ethics.
3. Christian ethics—Anglican authors.   4. Christian ethics—
Catholic authors.   I. Montefiore, Hugh.   II. Title.
BT708.d64 1989
241'.66—dc20   89–37786

British Library Cataloguing in Publication Data

Dominian, Jack, 1929–
    God, sex and love.
    1. Sex relations. Ethics – Christian viewpoints
    I. Title   II. Montefiore, Hugh, 1920–

ISBN 0–334–00533–7

NOV 1 1 1992

Typeset by J&L Composition Ltd, Filey, North Yorks
and printed in Great Britain by
Richard Clay Ltd, Bungay, Suffolk

Contents

Preface

Jack Dominian

In 1988 the Scottish University of Dundee invited us to give the Margaret Harris lectures on religion. We chose the field of sexual ethics which has been of enduring interest to both of us. As far as we know, this is the first time that a Roman Catholic and an Anglican have co-operated in this ecumenical way. Whilst differences remain between us, there is a shared belief that human behaviour, in this instance sexual ethics, should be the subject of moral examination with ethical implications, but that the law which emerges from these considerations should ultimately be subject to the supreme consideration of love as revealed in the gospel. This common approach could not disguise the fact that the subject of sexual morality is at a critical point, with marked differences between the churches and disagreements within individual churches. We believe that the lectures reflect this.

A total of five lectures were given. Bishop Montefiore introduced the subject of sexual ethics and dealt in particular with homosexuality, the field of abortion and *in vitro* fertilization. Dr Dominian dealt with masturbation and premarital sexual intercourse, marriage and marital breakdown. The contents are not exhaustive treatments of the subjects under consideration. They are summary introductions to a wide range of topical subjects which are not readily found in condensed forms. In this way we hope that they will be readily available to a wide range of non-specialists who want to acquaint themselves with current thought on these issues. We are conscious that the lectures were given in Britain and that the American scene was not specifically addressed. Nevertheless the issues dealt with are the same throughout Western society, and American readers should have little difficulty with the text.

In his introduction Bishop Montefiore laid the foundations for the course of lectures. He stressed that all human behaviour, in our case sexual ethics, has been subjected to the scrutiny of natural law, scripture and tradition. The Roman Catholic Church has emphasized the role of natural law and is heavily influenced by tradition. Protestants have left matters of behaviour to the individual judgment of lay people who are encouraged to decide for themselves in the light of the scriptures. In the past this has led to a predominance of law in Roman Catholic ethics with an accent on the personal in the Reformed tradition. Roman Catholics have been envious of the freedom of choice of Protestants and the latter eager to avail themselves of the more systematical conclusions of Roman Catholics. As in matters of scriptural exegesis, there has been a cross-fertilization, and both traditions are now emphasizing a morality based on the person and love. This is the approach we have shared in these lectures. It is a line of thought which ultimately lays great emphasis on conscience. The conscience of the individual has always been prominent in the Protestant tradition, and the Second Vatican Council also emphasized its importance, although for Roman Catholics it has to be fully informed by the Magisterium. Bishop Montefiore refers to practice in both traditions, whereby the objectivity of moral law has to be compensated by the flexibility of pastoral practice. Pastoral practice, based on God's love and forgiveness, gives succour to individuals who cannot fit their behaviour with the signs of the law. Such an approach makes the 'sinner' feel a second-rate citizen in the kingdom of God. Although human beings are always going to fall short of the demands of the gospel, there is a risk that conclusions on sexual ethics in the past laid unnecessary burdens, with unnecessary guilt, on men and women. There is a challenge not to dilute moral imperatives, but to ensure that men and women are not asked to conform to sexual behaviour which is unnecessarily strict and does not reflect the requirements of sexual integrity.

In the second lecture Dr Dominian takes up this challenge in matters of masturbation and premarital sexual intercourse. In the past, particularly under the shadow of St Augustine, sexual behaviour was only fully justified within marriage in its link with procreation. Western civilization has reached the point where the overwhelming majority of sexual acts within marriage are non-procreative. The intimate link between sexual intercourse and procreation has come to an end. This is allowing us to see that, as in all human behaviour, it is not the biological but love which gives the supreme value to human conduct. The functions of sex are assessed within an order of priority ranging from love, through procreation and sexual pleasure, to a relief of sexual tension that the orgasm gives. Both masturbation and coitus are freed from the prison of biology and examined against the background of the various meanings of sex. Masturbation is no longer considered a moral violation in adolescence and in many other situations. Marriage is seen as the proper perspective for sexual intercourse, not because sex is wrong before marriage and made right within it, but rather because marriage is a committed relationship of love which allows the conditions for the full expression of the richness of sex. In this context premarital sexual intercourse is examined in the light of its components in a committed relationship of love, and its morality is assessed in terms of commitment of love rather than being indicted uniformly as fornication.

The third lecture deals with marriage and marital breakdown. Throughout Judaeo-Christianity marriage has been accepted as a secular reality taken up in the divine order. The secular reality is principally seen as a relationship of love. Love is a word of multiple meanings. Dr Dominian describes two stages, that of 'falling in love', followed by 'loving'. Loving is described through sustaining, healing and growth. Marital breakdown, which is affecting between one in three and one in two of marriages in Western society, is seen as the major moral issue of our time, with major adverse consequences for the couple and the children. It is emphasized that our divorce-habituated society has yet to appreciate the immense damage and cost of marital breakdown, and the view is stressed that the churches should make the prevention of breakdown itself their priority rather than spending their main energies on how to handle its consequences. In the absence of any clear initiative from society or the churches to stem divorce, young people have taken to cohabitation as one way of preventing marital breakdown, but there is no evidence that this is a definitive answer to the problem. The various ways the churches handle marital breakdown is described with the view taken that none of them is satisfactory, but the Roman Catholic use of nullity is the most promising.

It is calculated that some ninety per cent of people marry. Research in the last fifty years has delineated one group of men and women who do not marry. These are homosexuals, and they constitute some five per cent of the community, easily the most common sexual minority. Until recently, homosexuals were subjected to the common hostility of society and the church. These people hid their sexual orientation for fear of censure, condemnation, loss of status and position. In the last twenty-five years there has been a determined effort to rehabilitate them, and this has raised an enormous amount of discussion in the Christian community. The Roman Catholic Church has remained adamant, and although it distinguishes between orientation and practice, even the former has been called 'a more or less strong tendency towards an intrinsic moral evil, and thus the inclination itself must be seen as an objective disorder'. Other churches are less condemnatory, but even so do not accept homosexual sexual activity as sexually moral. In the lecture Bishop Montefiore sets out the scriptural and natural law case against homosexuality, but nevertheless takes a positive view of the need of homosexuals for personal love and thus the formation of enduring, loving relationships.

In the last lecture Bishop Montefiore considers abortion and *in vitro* fertilization. As with divorce, the number of abortions has increased considerably in the last twenty years, and abortion, like divorce, has a controversial moral history which spans the whole Christian era. The positions taken by the churches differ. The Roman Catholic Church condemns all abortion, a position with which Dr Dominian identifies totally. The Church of England permits it when there is a grave threat to the physical and mental health of the mother. Bishop Montefiore agrees with this view, but readily admits that the overwhelming majority of abortions are carried out for personal reasons in women for whom the pregnancy is an inconvenience. The topic remains highly emotive and controversial, and the attempts to change the law continue at regular intervals.

Whilst an abortion constitutes the removal of a fertilized ovum, some eight to ten per cent of couples suffer from infertility. Here a number of new methods of fertilization have developed recently, culminating in *in vitro* fertilization. This is a complicated subject, still awaiting legal definition. *In vitro* fertilization raises a number of new moral issues which are dealt with by Bishop Montefiore in the second half of the lecture.

Between them, the subjects covered constitute the commonest issues in sexual ethics currently under discussion. At a time when AIDS is challenging the whole world to examine afresh its basis for sexual morality, the Christian position remains one of the principal voices which, while heeding and respecting the image of God in mankind, has to look afresh at the issues raised by sexuality. The growing diminution of biology as the basis for morality and the rise of personal love poses new issues in an area which affects all of us in our lives. The five lectures tackle these issues with a healthy respect for tradition and an urgent need to look at human sexuality afresh. Ultimately each person has to make choices dictated by the Christian conscience which collectively attempts to safeguard the image of God in man. This Christian conscience needs to speak increasingly with one voice to carry conviction. In these lectures the single voice has yet to be realized, but there is a growing consensus, and the excitement of attaining it has filled us both with the same hope that ecumenical endeavours are achieving in other fields.

This hope was only made possible by the vision of the University of Dundee, which gave us a free hand to attempt this goal of reconciliation. To all those involved in the invitation and for the welcome we received during our stay, our heartfelt thanks are extended. We hope that our imperfect initiative in Dundee may spread elsewhere and that the centre of Christendom, speaking with one voice on morals and ethics, may be realized in the not too distant future.

Introduction to Sexual Ethics

Hugh Montefiore

Human beings are unique because they are persons. They are not things, like inanimate material objects. They can be distinguished from the rest of the animal creation, and it is this uniqueness which gives to mankind its special dignity. In theological language we say that human beings are made in the image of God, so that they actually resemble God in certain ways; and further, that human personality has been hallowed by God through the incarnation of his Son in his assumption of human nature.

As we survey the wonderful panorama of biological evolution on this planet, from micro-organisms to man, we can see the beginnings – but only the beginnings – of our special characteristics in the higher mammals. Human beings have evolved in such a way that they have a moral sense of right and wrong. They are capable of reflective thought, and are able to engage in abstract reasoning. They can make a conscious choice between two courses of action. A human being is unique in being both the subject and object of his or her consciousness. Human beings are able consciously to worship their Creator. People, of course, are not alone in being able to communicate with one another. Animals also have means of communication, but this is much cruder than that of human beings, who through speech and language can communicate with great sophistication not only their feelings but also their thoughts and ideas. For this reason human beings are capable of uniquely close personal relationships.

For most people personal relationships constitute the most significant aspect of their lives. The highest human relationship is characterized by love. Christians believe that love is a reflection of the Divine Love, at the heart of which lies the mystery of the Holy Trinity. This is perhaps best described as the mystery of love between the three persons within God.

To understand our human nature, we have to see it in the context of the animal life from which it has evolved. Anthropologists have pointed out that some of our more irrational behaviour – hooliganism, for example, at football matches – may best be explained by reference to primaeval tribal or even prehuman behaviour. In the animal kingdom, there is often a preoccupation with reproductive behaviour, without which a species could not continue; and often, too, a struggle by a male to achieve sexual dominance, a struggle whose results promote the well being of the species. In certain animals, bonding occurs between a male and a female of the species, sometimes for a period, sometimes for life. Their cooperation is essential for the survival of their young if the female is preoccupied with hatching eggs or caring for her brood. Animals may also display what seems to us to be intelligent behaviour, but they are incapable of choice and self-knowledge. They act in accordance with blind instinctual urges and they are not capable of a close personal relationship.

We human beings retain our animal nature. We find many traces of our animal past in human behaviour, not least in sexual matters, as in courting displays and struggles for male dominance. Males tend to prefer young and attractive spouses, who are more likely to be fertile; while females tend to prefer older and successful spouses, who are more likely to provide a secure home in which to rear children. We ignore our animal nature at our peril, because this means we lack self-knowledge, and this is always dangerous.

But human beings also ignore at their peril their own unique and distinctive characteristics. The love which unites a couple is not just the natural bonding which occurs for the procreation of children: it is also a deep personal relationship which involves not just the feelings, but the whole personality, including the mind and the will. The primitive sexual bonding of animals is only the base on which human love is built. The mutual love of two people far transcends it. Shakespeare wrote in Sonnet 116:

> Let me not to the marriage of true minds
> Admit impediments. Love is not love
> Which alters when it alteration finds,
> Or bends with the remover to remove.
> O, no! It is an ever-fixed mark,
> That looks on tempests and is never shaken.

Love like that is not susceptible of a purely chemical explanation: it is a window into the very nature of God.

Among those human characteristics that can be called unique is the ability to make conscious and informed choices. Humankind may not always agree on what is right and wrong; but people know that some intentions are good and some are bad. They are responsible for their actions and they know that some of these are right and some are wrong. This holds good for human relationships: some are good and some are bad. Human relationships include sex and love. Because our bodies and souls interact, the two can never be wholly separated. Our sexual urges are derived from our primitive nature: they may be blind and they are often very strong. They need to be regulated. If follows that mankind needs a morality of sex, what we call sexual ethics.

It is with sexual ethics that this book is concerned. It is written by an Anglican and a Roman Catholic, a theologian and a psychiatrist. Dr Dominian, as a consultant psychiatrist of great distinction, will naturally be emphasizing psychological factors, while I shall be more concerned with theological aspects. We shall both give, as faithfully as we can, the teaching of one another's churches as well as of our own, both where they agree and where they disagree; and we shall at the same time make clear what we think ourselves.

Although this book is about sexual ethics, a distinction must first be made between the Christian gospel and Christian ethics. The gospel is about God, about how God treats us; while ethics is about human beings, about how they should behave. The gospel of Jesus Christ is not primarily about being good, nor about any other moralism. It is about God. In England, where Christianity is often thought to be about being a decent fellow and leading a good life, that needs to be emphasized, but perhaps not so much elsewhere. In fact Jesus went out of his way to preach the gospel to those who were not commonly regarded as good fellows, and who were certainly not leading good lives. He never relaxed his moral standards for them; but he did not start by telling them how bad they were. He befriended them and told them the Good News, that God loved them and cared for them and forgave them. Human behaviour springs from the kind of people we are; and the gospel is about changing our nature and enabling us to be the kind of people we are meant to be.

Until our nature is changed, it is impossible for us to change our interior attitudes, and it is with interior attitudes that Jesus was primarily concerned. With iron self-control, a person may be able to regulate his or her outward behaviour without such interior change. This applies to sexual behaviour as much as to other kinds of human behaviour. But a person's interior dispositions remain unchanged, and may, for example, manifest themselves in the more bizarre kinds of sexual fantasy. Self-discipline cannot by itself change lust into love; and lust falls under condemnation in the teaching of Jesus. But not lustful people. 'Neither do I condemn you,' Jesus said to the woman taken in the act of adultery, 'Go and sin no more.' This well illustrates the difference between gospel and law. The law condemns adultery, as for example in the Ten Commandments. The gospel, however, does not condemn the adulterer, yet this lack of condemnation in no way diminishes the rigour of the law's demands. God in his love accepts us in all our unacceptability.

The fact that we are accepted in this way by God enables us both to accept ourselves and to forgive other people. Since our human wills and affections are so often unruly, our sexual behaviour as a consequence often 'misses the mark', and so there will be occasions when we need to forgive ourselves and to accept forgiveness from a loved one as well as to extend it to others in matters of sex.

The love of God which has resulted in God's acceptance of all men and women as sons and daughters has two main aspects, reflected in the Greek words *agape* and *eros*. *Agape* involves a determination of the will to help and support at all costs the object of our love. It is, if you like, unselfish love. It is perhaps best illustrated by the famous text from St John's Gospel: 'God so loved the world that he gave his only begotten Son to the end that all that believe in him should not perish but have everlasting life.'

A second important aspect of human love is *eros*, the passionate desire to be united with the beloved. St Augustine, probably writing out of his own pre-conversion experience, seems to have regarded this kind of love as *concupiscentia*, something entailed on humankind by the Fall. He was only prepared not to condemn it because it was inescapable in order to achieve the 'good' of procreation. In this respect St Augustine cast a long shadow over human sexuality in Western Christendom, from which it has only recently been recovering. In fact *eros*, the passionate desire to be united with the beloved, is part of God's gift to humanity, provided that it is combined with *agape*, the determination of the lover to cherish the beloved with tenderness and affection, and to provide support, help and comfort.

Agape is always used in the New Testament both of God's love and of the human response. Can we also attribute *eros* to God's own self? I believe we can. *Agape* is used exclusively in the New Testament because its pages are preoccupied with the costly and sacrificial love of God shown in Christ's saving death upon the cross. But it is also true that God yearns over us. God has not only acted self-sacrificially through Christ for our fulfilment and welfare, but also passionately desires to unite us to himself. In the same kind of way, when two people love one another deeply, each of them desires the welfare and happiness of the other, and also at the same time yearns for their mutual union. Human love between two persons is a reflection of God's love. Indeed, it often forms the means by which the two people concerned first become aware of God's love for them both.

The fact that two people love one another does not mean that they may do whatever they may feel like to express that love. Sexual intercourse between two people is a most intimate act, involving self-donation between two persons which penetrates to the very centre of their being. A loving relationship between such two persons, if it is to be expressed by such an act of total self-giving, 'misses the mark' unless it is adequate for that expression. It should be characterized by commitment (for it includes *agape* as well as *eros*, involving not just the feelings, but the whole person). The relationship needs to be exclusive (for total self-giving can only be made to one other person); and it needs to be permanent (for if it is not permanent, it cannot be total). Because sexual drives are urgent and powerful, it is necessary for their proper control that society should have rules of behaviour for the sexual conduct of individuals. Some of these rules require the enforcement of the civil law for the protection of people against sexual abuse. Most of them, however, consist of laws of personal behaviour binding upon the conscience of individuals.

Some actions are expedient and some are inexpedient. Some actions are in principle right and other are in principle wrong. Some are right for me or for you, and others are wrong for me or for you. How do we determine what is right or wrong?

To rely simply on our own personal moral reasoning and intuition is dangerous. Although we have a natural sense of right and wrong, and although we are promised help from the Holy Spirit of God, yet we are all, alas, far from perfect, and we are only too apt to give ourselves the benefit of the doubt in these matters. For all the God-givenness of reason, it is as subject to corruption as any other aspect of our personality. There is, however, a vital source of assistance. We are members of the church. We share in its common life, and we need to know and should hope to share its common mind on matters of conduct, including sexual conduct. In other words, we need to inform our conscience.

How do we do that? There are three main ways. In the first place, there is what is called the natural law. This is a vague term, and for that reason distrusted by many. Furthermore, the phrase can refer to different kinds of argument.

1. The natural law is often thought to consist of general principles of conduct which are generally known and accepted. An example of this might be that 'a greater good is to be preferred to a lesser evil'. Again, it is natural for human beings to desire social intercourse and friendship, and to exercise freedom of the will and freedom of conscience: these are normative among human beings, and they show the existence of a natural law and natural rights. The trouble about such generalizations is that they are far too general to regulate conduct. They can give us little guidance so far as sexual ethics are concerned.

2. Another way of looking at the natural law is to consider those institutions which society has evolved and which are universally or almost universally supported by all human societies. Marriage could be an example of this approach. It is a natural state of life, and it is often regarded as part of the natural law for humankind. This is shown by the need of a man and a woman for mutual support, as well as by the need of a secure base for the rearing of children. It is also evidenced by the almost universal importance and protection afforded to the institution of marriage in all societies. In addition, there are very generally diffused sexual tabus to protect marriage, such as those against incest or for the prohibition of bestialism. However these tabus may have originated – and there is no certainty on this – it is in the interests of society as a whole that they be regarded as morally binding on its members. These arguments in favour of marriage as a natural law carry considerable weight; but they hardly achieve full conviction. Not all societies have rules for the protection of monogamous marriages. For the continuance of our race it is hardly necessary for *everyone* to marry. Not everyone requires the support of a spouse for their well being. In the pluralist societies of the West it is very difficult to discern institutions which are universally accepted and approved.

3. There is a third way of looking at the natural law which carries much more weight. The world of nature has evolved in accordance with natural laws and constants. The natural sciences, in the more recent past, have been amazingly successful in investigating these regularities and in providing explanations of why things are as they are. But we cannot find out by these investigations how human beings ought to behave.

Is it possible to consider any circumstances in which we can derive what ought to be the case from what is the case? When we turn to consider the human body, we find that certain organs have evolved for certain functions. The human arm and hand, for example, which may have originally developed to assist our animal ancestors in swinging from branch to branch, have subsequently evolved so that they have become instruments of great skills and dexterity for the fulfilment of manual tasks. Our legs, on the other hand, have developed so as to assist our mobility as bipedal mammals. If our legs unfortunately become useless, it may be necessary, in a primitive society, to use our arms and hands as very inferior substitutes to achieve mobility. But, while it would be just possible, it would be unnatural, indeed contrary to the natural law of our being, for us generally to walk with our hands. In the same way it could be said to be unnatural, and contrary to the natural law of our being, to use organs which have evolved for reasons of reproduction and unitive love between a man and a woman for purposes other than those for which they have evolved.

Natural law, in whatever sense it may be used, is not a universal and clear guide to human conduct, and that includes human sexual conduct. An ethic based solely on such a source would be in need of clarification and precision. Christians have two sources for this; scripture and tradition.

The scriptures are a source of very great authority, and this authority is universally acknowledged throughout Christendom. However, the precise degree of authority to be attached to particular writings in the scriptures needs considerable care and discrimination. Old Testament morality, for example, needs to be assessed in the light of New Testament teaching; and New Testament teaching needs to be considered in the context of the culture of the primitive church and in the light of new knowledge which may be available today. The teaching attributed to Jesus will carry a special authority, but at the same time the possibility that in some cases that teaching has been amended or supplemented by the author of a Gospel, or by the tradition which he represents, cannot be ruled out. Furthermore, there are cases when there are apparent contradictions in the teaching of Jesus, for example when the Gospel of St Matthew is compared with those of St Mark and St Luke on the subject of divorce. Again, it is dangerous to treat the sayings of Jesus as though he were intending to lay down laws of human conduct. What might appear today to us to be exaggerated statements, if we take them literally, in his day would have been regarded as vivid ways of inculcating moral truths (for example, his command to tear out an eye which causes offence).

These considerations might at first sight make it seem as though the authority of the New Testament on matters of sexual conduct (as indeed on other matters of human behaviour) has been eroded. But this is by no means the case. Where we find repetition within the Gospels and corroboration between the Gospels, a saying of Jesus has particular force. For example, we have no reason whatsoever to doubt that Jesus taught that marriage is intended to be permanent. The authority of the New Testament is such that we need to be certain that a sexual issue has been radically affected by new circumstances or by new knowledge before we can amend its teachings.

In addition to the scriptures we have the authoritative teaching of the churches. Other heads are likely to be wiser than our own, and the guidance of the Holy Spirit has been promised to the whole fellowship of believers. At the same time, authoritative church teaching suffers from the limitation that it can only be in the form of generalizations, which take no account of particular cases, and especially of our particular case. What is more, church teaching is not necessarily final. The Anglican churches hold that mistakes can be made even by ecumenical councils. The Anglican record on artificial contraception, as shown in the resolutions of successive Lambeth Conferences, affords a good illustration of how Anglican teaching can develop and change in the light of altered circumstances (the overpopulation of the world) and of a deeper understanding of marriage (in terms of the stewardship of resources in a family and of the unitive function of sex within marriage).

The Roman Catholic Church puts great emphasis on continuity with its past: yet it is not altogether impervious to change. Its teaching can also show development, as has happened over its understanding of the unitive as well as the procreative functions of sex within marriage. Although the doctrine of papal infallibility in matters of faith and morals was defined at Vatican I, there is no decree by a Pope (or for that matter by an ecumenical council) on sexual matters for which infallibility has been claimed, although of course pronouncements and statements by local bishops, by the Vatican Congregation for the Doctrine of the Faith, and of course by the Pope himself, carry great authority for members of that church.

Today we live in a time of great change, in which we are faced with decisions in areas for which neither the scriptures nor past tradition can give us any direct teaching, and in which the natural law gives no clear guidance. We are faced with new situations and with deeper knowledge in many areas concerning sexual behaviour. Moral theologians need to apply afresh their principles of moral theology to these new matters, and the laity have an important contribution to make in areas of their own expertise, especially in churches which have a celibate clergy. In the complex world of technological innovation the hierarchy may not always have a ready answer to the moral questions posed by such innovations. But in view of uncertainties felt by church members, church authorities may feel called upon to make fresh pronouncements on aspects of sexual ethics. Individual church people ought to be aware of those that are relevant to their own situation. Unless they have good and strong reasons for withholding their consent to such teaching, they have an obligation to receive it.

The Protestant churches have a tendency to individualism, and they have been chary of issuing such pronouncements. They have given priority to the new life in Christ, given for all those who have died and risen again in him. This new life should issue in a purity of intention to live in accordance with God's will. So the Protestant churches, generally speaking, have left such matters of behaviour to the private judgment of their lay people for them to make up their own minds in the light of scriptural teaching. They have been more concerned with the broad field of Christian ethics than with details of moral theology.

There is a certain fluidity in terminology that is used in this connection; but we may say that Christian ethics dealt with Christian behaviour, while moral theology is more concerned with the principles on which Christian behaviour should be based. Behind moral theology lies the discipline of moral philosophy, that is to say, thinking about the principles of morality and moral behaviour, taking into account the moral intention of an agent, the moral nature of an act, and the probable consequences of the act. Moral philosophers often think of these probable consequences as the only criteria for morality; but such a view is clearly insufficient for Christians, who may hold to the natural law, and who accept the authority of scripture and tradition, and who recognize a call to personal holiness of life.

Moral theology ought to be regarded as a branch of theology, intimately related to its other branches. For example, so far as sexual ethics are concerned, moral theology ought to be related to spiritual theology, so that it is relevant to a person's prayer life, as well as to dogmatic theology, so that it is relevant to a person's redemption and salvation. Moral theology ought to explore the practical implications of our commitment to Jesus Christ in the sphere (among others) of sexual behaviour. In fact it has tended to become legalistic, resulting in general ethical statements derived deductively from agreed principles and issued by church authorities.

Such statements require application to particular cases. The Roman Catholic code of canon law achieves this to a limited extent. Moral case studies involve a more detailed consideration of particular cases: they belong to a branch of moral theology known as casuistry. This has become a 'boo' word, since it fell into disrepute in the sixteenth and seventeenth centuries, owing to the 'permissiveness' which could be justified by some casuistical methods. But there is a good side to casuistry. Situations and people differ, and casuistry evolved precisely to meet the complexity of people's ethical dilemmas, including the moral issues of sex.

In the early days of the church, and especially in the Middle Ages, lists were made (called 'penitentials') of different kinds of sins, with varying degrees of penance appropriate for each. Moral theology has been mostly concerned with sins, and after the Council of Trent, when confession became obligatory, guidance was required for priests in the confessional. Inevitably consideration was given to various forms of sexual sin. At first sight this concern with penances seems to ignore the basic call of the gospel for faith. Over-emphasis on 'mortal sins' seems to deny the overriding importance of what has been called 'the fundamental option' (i.e., the fundamental choice of individuals for God, and their basic disposition towards God, in the light of which those details of their lives where they have 'missed the mark' seem of much lesser importance). But these penitentials, for all their shortcomings, served a useful purpose. They were 'a realistic acknowledgment of types of all too common human predicaments, and an awareness of the fact that law, even God's, does not automatically answer every query, but that for many much of life is a series of worried "But, what ifs"?'[1]

As casuistry developed, different principles emerged which were adopted by different systems for deciding between behaviour choices in particular cases. Probabilism did not mean what it seems. It is not the principle that the option which is more likely to be right should be chosen. It is derived from the Latin *probabilis*, provable; and under the casuistical system of probabilism, any option that is provable, that is to say, that can be rationally justified, is acceptable. This opened the door to justifying plainly immoral behaviour.

Probabiliorism is the principle that the option that is more likely to be rationally justified should be taken, while aequiprobabilism is the principle that one could take either of two options that seem equally balanced. The principle most adopted by the church has been tutiorism, that the safer option must be taken. (Once, however, the church has pronounced on a sexual matter, Roman Catholic teaching is that individuals are bound to accept this, unless they have weighty and what are to them conclusive objections to so doing.)

One of the results of this kind of casuistry has been to understand Christian behaviour in terms of moral law, so that we tend to think exclusively of what is objectively right and what is objectively wrong, what is permitted and what is forbidden. Useful as this is, it tends to overshadow the gospel, which is about love and not about law. The gospel requires the voluntary response of the human heart: the law requires the duty of obedience and submission. The love of God revealed in Christ invites us to take 'the fundamental option' of responding to this love by deciding for God, whereas the law tends to distance us from God by concentrating on our failures. The law is concerned with the minutiae of behaviour; but the gospel addresses the whole person in terms of renewal and forgiveness and in its call for faith.

love vs. law

There is a considerable field for casuistry when marriages break up. Was the original marriage a 'real' marriage or not? On this question, according to Catholic principles, turns the question whether 'remarriage' is permissible during the lifetime of a former spouse. Certain formal conditions must be satisfied before the first marriage can be considered null and void. These conditions do not seem to take into account the personal predicament of the people involved. They are concerned with the formal assessment of intentions and actions in the light of agreed principles and precedents, a form of legalism which may seem far removed from the spirit of gospel teaching.

To criticize moral theology in this way should not be understood so as to depreciate many of its achievements. We do need moral principles of action on which to base behaviour. We need to be able to state quite categorically whether we think that a particular action is, in principle, right or wrong; and we must not pull our punches. Unless this is done, it will seem that our moral standards are hazy, or even that we do not care very much about them. It is necessary to clear the air, as it were, and to enable church people to have clear goals and ideals, and it makes it possible for people outside the church to know what its standards are.

But at the same time, in trying to help people, we must start from where they actually are. We must not look at matters simply in the abstract. We need equally to consider the real personal dilemma with which an actual person is confronted, at a particular time in his or her life, living within a particular culture. We must appreciate that while some actions may have been condemned by the church on the grounds of some perfectly valid principle, this principle may be opposed by some other principle which seems equally, or perhaps even more important to the person actually concerned. We must ask ourselves not only whether a particular option is in principle right or wrong, but whether in this or that situation this option is more right for the individual person concerned than another option which involves another important principle which may seem to override it.

To say this is not to accept the principles of 'situation ethics', which do away with objective morality altogether, and according to which everyone in his or her situation will be able to make their own loving response to each situation without considering any principle other than love. We may acknowledge 'the Christian instincts of the faithful and the upright moral consciousness of men',[2] but such acknowledgment does not lead us to suppose that God always illuminates everyone so that they automatically know the right response they ought to make to each situation. We do need norms of Christian behaviour considered in abstract, providing that we realize that they are not to be applied simplistically to the actual complex situations in which individuals may find themselves.

The church has tried to make provision for a more flexible approach in various ways. One of these was casuistry, the

disadvantages of which we have already noted. A second approach
has been through its teachings on conscience.

What is conscience? The definition of conscience in the Vatican
constitution *Gaudium et Spes* is not very satisfactory. There it is
described as 'the most secret core and sanctuary of a man. There he
is alone with God, whose voice echoes in his depths.' The
constitution continues:

> In the depths of his conscience, man detects a law which he does
> not impose on himself, but which holds him to obedience.
> Always summoning him to love good and to avoid evil, the voice
> of conscience can when necessary speak to his heart more
> specifically: do this, shun that. For man has in his heart a law
> written by God. To obey it is the very dignity of man: according
> to it he will be judged.[3]

The difficulty about this way of considering conscience is that it
suggests that there is a particular faculty of the mind or soul of
human beings, their 'secret core and sanctuary', which distinguishes conscience from the rest of their personality. Again, the
wording of the constitution suggests that conscience, as a law, is
the 'new law of love' written in human hearts by God. But the
phrase 'law of love' is at best paradoxical, and suggests that
submission to law is of the essence of conscience.

Is there a more satisfactory way of regarding conscience?
Conscience is best thought of as the result of a person's deepest
moral reflections on actual situations. Conscience will often be the
result of the mind consciously applying itself to these situations,
thinking morally about the personal choices confronting a person.
But conscience may not always be the result of articulate moral
reasoning. Sometimes it may be inarticulate, because a person's
moral principles can be deeply imbedded in his or her unconscious
sentiments. Individuals confronted by some moral choice (e.g.,
whether or not to remarry while a former spouse is still living) may
'feel in their bones' that one choice is right for them: they are
'conscience-bound' to take it.

It is not always realized that, according to Catholic as well as

Protestant theology, conscience must be obeyed. Certainly in the
Roman Catholic Church the 'faithful' are told to submit themselves
to the teaching of their bishops and of course to that of the Supreme
Pontiff. They owe obedience to what is called the 'ordinary
magisterium' of the church. But at the same time the possibility of
conscientious objection is recognized. It is the duty of a man or a
woman to follow their conscience, even in those cases where
conscience is culpably mistaken, because to do otherwise would be
tantamount to refusing to do what was perceived to be the will of
God. In such a case individuals are not merely free to follow their
consciences: they are bound to do so. They may have to suffer the
consequences of following their consciences, because it may lead
them to transgress the laws of the state or the regulations of their
church: nonetheless they have a duty to obey. Conscience thus
plays a very important role in moral decision-making in all
churches, whether in the Protestant or Catholic traditions.

Human beings, however, are not merely responsible *to* their
consciences: they are also responsible *for* their consciences. When
individuals' consciences diverge from the authoritative teaching of
the church, they have a duty to inform themselves of the church's
teaching, weighing it with all seriousness, and they are only
justified in deciding to act in accordance with their own private
judgment after hard thought and deep self-examination. But if
they still continue in their convictions, they have a duty to act by
them, in sexual as in other matters.

In addition to casuistry and conscience, there is a third way by
which the church has introduced some flexibility into its moral
thinking. This is by means of a distinction between moral and
pastoral theology. The church has accepted St Augustine's principle that God always gives sufficient grace for us to accomplish
that which he demands. It follows, therefore, that if some are
unable to meet in full moral demands in any area of ethics,
including sexual ethics, then there has to be a pastoral solution to this dilemma. For example, it is no use commanding those
who suffer from compulsive behaviour to cease from their com-
pulsions because these involve activity that is objectively wrong.

Speaking in moral terms, such behaviour is wrong; but in pastoral terms, such people are not fully responsible for all their actions. They cannot be expected voluntarily to desist from behaviour which is compulsive. They cannot be blamed if they are unable to do what they ought to do. Perhaps they might be blamed for having allowed themselves to get into such a state, if in fact they are responsible for their present situation; but that is another matter.

In the same kind of way, it is sometimes no use telling people with interior problems to pull themselves together and to use their willpower so that they do not succumb to temptation. I personally appreciated the 'stiff upper lip' of military discipline: it helped me in difficult situations during the Second World War. But in more normal circumstances this kind of approach can be very sterile. What people need is an interior change of their deepest sentiments; and these are best changed through relationships rather than through discipline. The affect of a loving relationship is more potent in this regard that any amount of moralizing in terms of objective moral theology. Pastoral theology has accepted these points; and pastors are exhorted to deal sensitively with penitents, to be careful not to hold people culpable when this is not appropriate, and to use 'prudent judgment'.

At the same time pastoral theology, used in this way, tends to become a 'theology of the second-best', a loophole for the weak, a softening of the demands of moral theology. Professor Mahoney has described the situation as follows:

This traditional distinction between the 'moral' and the 'pastoral' approach leads inevitably to an impoverished view of both moral theology and pastoral theology. It accentuates in moral theology an approach which is concerned exclusively with universals rather than with particulars, and it lends itself too readily to the elaboration of theology in terms of the law as 'normal' and of anything else as requiring justification through the exploring of exceptions to the law ... In those Church members who, for one reason or another, are unable to 'measure

up' to the universal norms of moral theology, such pastoral concern and sympathetic understanding, while often undoubtedly
helpful, can also at the same confirm or reinforce a personal
sense of failure, delinquency, and hopelessness which is terrible
to contemplate.[4]

What is required is a way of doing moral theology which does not
neglect objective principles, but which also takes into account the
actual situation of a person, not by way of concession, but as a vital
and necessary ingredient in coming to a decision about the right
course of Christian behaviour for a particular individual. Such an
approach is specially needed in sexual ethics, for in this area there
are many private 'hang-ups' and situations unique to the individuals concerned.

Sometimes people, by a wrong course of action, have involved
themselves in an impossible situation. They may find themselves landed with responsibilities from which it would be immoral to walk away, however much the judgments of objective
moral theology might seem to demand this. By carrying out
these responsibilities they may be, objectively speaking, doing
wrong; and they may be aware of this. And yet they may be
aware that by reneging on these responsibilities they would be
letting down another person in a way that offends their conscience
still more. None of us would find it very difficult to imagine a
situation of this kind affecting the intimate relations of three
people.

Sometimes people are just immature and are unable to behave in
a mature way. Sometimes their moral judgment has been swamped
or warped by the strength of their emotional feelings; and those
feelings are not at their command. They need time to grow up, to
cool off, to reflect, before they can fully respond to what may be
demanded of them. This applies not only to teenagers, but also to
those of riper years. Such people, like the prodigal son, need time
and space in a far country, in order to come to themselves. In such
cases a loving and understanding relationship is likely to be more
helpful than the objective requirements of the moral law, which are

likely to induce feelings of guilt and thus make the situation worse than it is already.

It may be necessary to choose between two evils. It is sometimes not possible to refrain from doing something without causing a worse evil than if one had not done it. The stock instance of this is the telling of a lie. Truth is required by the gospel and hallowed by tradition. It is also demanded by the natural law, since lying is parasitic on truth, in the sense that we must presume that people are telling the truth or social intercourse becomes impossible. But if the proverbial lunatic, brandishing a knife, enquired of me which direction a person he was pursuing had taken, I would be fully justified in responding with a lie, hoping that when it was discovered that it was a lie, the lunatic would not return and plunge his knife into me!

This is an extreme case; but there are circumstances when in making a choice in matters of sexual ethics individuals may find that in the actual situation in which they find themselves, the choice is neither black or white, but grey: a choice between two courses, to both of which there are moral objections.

choices in sexual ethics

Moral theology ought to give weight to subjective factors as well as to objective principles of behaviour. This is not to water down the demands of the gospel, which are infinite. They call for heroism, determination and self-sacrifice. There are certainly individuals who are called to fulfil them literally; like St Anthony of Alexandria, who, when he walked out of church, gave away all he possessed and went into the desert. It is incumbent upon all of us to respond to the limit of our abilities. The great American theologian Reinhold Niebuhr accurately described these demands of the gospel as 'impossible possibilities'. We dare not give ourselves the benefit of the doubt in deciding that it is not for us to take them literally. But at the same time they are not applicable to each and everyone's situation. Since we can never know the full story, both outward and inward, of any one else's situation, we have to leave it to their own informed conscience for them to know what is the right thing for them to do in their own particular case.

There are some indications in the gospel that Jesus himself

accepted this. He is reported to have shattered his disciples by saying: 'It is easier for a camel to pass through the eye of a needle than for a rich man to enter into the Kingdom of Heaven.' Many attempts have been made to dilute the meaning of this saying; but it had sufficient impact on the disciples for them to enquire: 'Then who can be saved?' Jesus looked on them and said, 'For men this is impossible, but everything is possible with God.' He did not thereby withdraw the full rigour of his saying: the principle remains. At the same time he suggests that God, in judging individuals, will know their full story, and will recognize that there are particular situations in which the saying does not apply literally.

Another such instance occurs in Jesus's sweeping condemnation of all remarriage after divorce, which made such an impact on his disciples that they exclaimed: 'If that is the position between husband and wife, it is better not to marry.' To this Jesus replied: 'This is not something which everyone can accept, but only those for whom God has appointed it.' There is no toning down of the objective principle, but he spoke of Moses permitting divorce 'for the hardness of your hearts', as though this were something inevitable. This seems to suggest that people can only do what is possible, and that there will be those for whom remarriage is the only possible solution.

It seems, therefore, that we can find in the Gospels some support for the view that God's infinite demand must be seen in the context of an individual's actual personal situation. This is an approach which I will be using in considering homosexuality, abortion and new techniques for human fertilization. Dr Dominian, who will be speaking about masturbation, premarital sexual behaviour, marriage and marital breakdown, will be concentrating on psychological aspects; but I think that these considerations will also be relevant to what he has to say.

Sexual matters are very intimate for all of us, because this is an area of life where we are all vulnerable and which involves the feelings rather than the mind. We shrink from moral discourse about it other than in terms of generalization because this would involve us in laying open the very depths of our being. Sex is sacramental, in the sense that our bodily actions express our deepest attitudes and our strongest commitments. Sex, after all, has evolved for the deepest mysteries of all, the transmission of life and the union of two persons in love. Sex is not only for many their greatest source of God-given pleasure, but it is also of central concern for their personal happiness. It can also cause great anxiety, and some of mankind's deepest unhappiness. Sex can absorb a great deal of a person's interior life. Even more important, it enables a person to realize his or her deepest identity. For these reasons sex gathers round itself many tabus, conventions, prejudices, fantasies and fears.

It is therefore necessary to be realistic in discussing sexual ethics. We must not dilute Christian ideals and Christian teaching. But we have to deal with actual situations in which human beings are called to act with integrity. Human well-being must be our goal, with real compassion for the unhappy. Personal moral qualities matter most. God has shown that love is more basic than law.

2

Masturbation and Premarital Sexual Intercourse

Jack Dominian

Introduction

The subjects of masturbation and premarital sexual intercourse have fascinated both moralists and doctors. In the nineteenth century masturbation was held to cause madness. In the Roman Catholic tradition to which I belong both matters have been of immense importance. I grew up with a religious awareness that they were forbidden and indeed were serious moral violations. In this chapter I want to examine the nature of sexuality, the changing norms of the last twenty-five years and the specific moral issues.

In the Christian tradition of all denominations is to be found the shadow of St Augustine with his own personal history of sexuality coupled with the Epicurean and Stoic backgrounds of ancient Greece. At the heart of all these philosophers lies the treatment of pleasure in general and sexual pleasure in particular. St Augustine, whose own obsession with sexuality undoubtedly shaped his teaching which has been influential ever since, experienced sexual pleasure as highly attractive, holding him spellbound for a long period of his youth. At a later stage and as a reaction, he taught that the only justification for sexual intercourse was its link with pro-creation in marriage. The struggle to rehabilitate sexual pleasure as an entity has challenged theologians ever since Augustine, and the story is well documented in Noonan's book *Contraception*.[1] In the last quarter of a century we have witnessed in the permissive society of the West one of the final and decisive chapters of this debate.

The advent of the contraceptive pill in 1960 produced a major social and sexual revolution. For the first time in the history of humankind a relatively safe and highly effective contraceptive was found that could be handled by women. This effectively separated sexual intercourse from procreation. The fact is that whatever method of birth regulation is used, currently ninety-nine per cent of sexual activity is knowingly and deliberately non-procreative. Even within marriage, most couples need only a few sexual acts to achieve their desired family size. So the pill and other modern methods of birth regulation have precipitated anew the perennial question of the meaning of sexual intercourse, which is the basic issue that has to be addressed prior to considering sexual ethics in the matters of masturbation and premarital sex.

The Freudian revolution

The roots of sexual ethics had been laid down prior to the Freudian revolution. Before Freud, sexual pleasure began with puberty and was associated with the secondary sexual characteristics of boys and girls; indeed masturbation was heralded as its first manifestation.

The Freudian and more specifically the psychodynamic tradition has changed this view of sexuality and has placed it in the life of the child from the moment it is born. Freud described instinctual, libidinal pleasure in the baby, locating it in the mouth, anus, and the infantile genitals. We do not have to be Freudians to appreciate that the mouth and the anus are lined with a smooth mucous membrane which is pleasurable to touch and that young children have masturbatory experiences. In other words, sexual pleasure clearly predates puberty.

Even more important than this Freudian description of the anatomical sites of sexual pleasure, the psychoanalytical tradition has defined another dimension which has profound implications for sexuality.

Freud believed that the human personality was based on the development and vicissitudes of the two instincts of aggression and sexuality. In his theory the person who dealt with the baby, usually the mother, was the target for the discharge of these instincts.

Very soon another psychoanalytical school emerged which saw the mother, not as an object of instinctual discharge, but as the essential person with whom the child interacted for its development. This interaction was both instinctual and loving. This school of thought has been embraced by all psychoanalysis and is called object-relations theory.[2] Object-relations theory has profound implications for sexuality. It means that all of us have, from the moment we are born, a relationship with our parental figures which combines instinct and love. As we grow up we learn, in our interaction with our parents, to feel recognized, wanted and appreciated. Alternatively, we feel ignored, unwanted, neglected or unappreciated. These experiences of childhood are absolutely fundamental in appreciating the ultimate meaning of sexuality. If we are to remain within the framework of what is natural, in other words what is human, then instinct and love are joined together in a unity which at its best captures the wholeness of human experience. In other words, adult sexuality is much more than mere expression of instinct so beloved of many theologians of a previous generation. When we make love as adults we are reacting to more than a body; we are responding to a person. How we respond to that person depends on how we experienced our parents and ourselves as children. If we felt appreciated and loved we are beckoned in sexual intercourse by someone who has similar feelings of affirmation. If we were neglected as children it is easy to feel that the person who is making love to us only wants our body and does not love us as a person. The way we were treated as children makes an enormous difference to how we interact in sexual intercourse because we relive with the person with whom we are making love the most intimate experiences of our childhood. This is absolutely fundamental in appreciating the ultimate meaning of sexuality. If we are to remain within the framework of what is natural, in other words what is human, then instinct and love are joined together in a unity which at its best captures the wholeness of human experience.

To this very day so many theorists assert that there is no link between sexual pleasure and love that it is important to have a full understanding of human nature in which the two are essentially linked. This link is the answer to pursuing sexual pleasure separately from a personal interaction of love. But if the hedonist needs correction, so does the Christian fundamentalist who sees the essential link to be between sex and procreation, as the Catholic Church still teaches us in the encyclical *Humanae Vitae*.[3] This tradition has yet to learn that before sex was linked with procreation, it was connected with personal love in the depths of interpersonal communication.

In referring to *Humanae Vitae* it is vital to remind ourselves that this remains the official teaching of the Roman Catholic Church. The fact is that the overwhelming majority of Roman Catholic moral theologians and the faithful have rejected this teaching and there is a continuous tension between the teaching authority and the rest of the Roman Catholic community. The essence of the teaching depends on the view that there is an essential link between sexual intercourse and procreation which must not be denied. At the heart of this view is an instinctual, biological view of sexual intercourse which in the light of all I have said is inconsistent with reality. At the centre of sexual intercourse is a duality of biology and personal love, and of the two the latter has always the overwhelming priority. This does not mean that contraception cannot be misused. It can and frequently is, in the sense that it is used to offer a safeguard against fertilization in the absence of a loving encounter. But the fact that contraception can be misused does not render it invalid in the proper circumstances when it is used to facilitate love (for a detailed discussion on the subject see my book *Sexual Integrity*).[4]

From this it follows that the most basic characteristic in the human personality is the link between sexual pleasure and personal

love. The separation of the two is the acting out of the basic
alienation in the human person. Sex and love are related for
everybody and not just Christians.

Puberty

Puberty is the time of the arrival of the secondary sexual
characteristics with the potential of adult sexual intercourse,
procreation and the intensity of orgastic pleasure, either spontaneously or induced. Induced sexual pleasure with or without
orgasm is referred to as masturbation.

Before dealing with masturbation, let us summarize the characteristics of sexual outlet. Sexual activity has the potential first and
foremost of being linked with love in a relationship with another
person. In this respect it is life-giving to those involved. Secondly,
it has the capacity of fertilization, which means the start of a new
life. Thirdly, it is accompanied by an intense pleasure which
reaches its peak at orgasm. Fourthly, though this is often
forgotten, orgasm is accompanied by relief of sexual tension.

Therefore an ethic which wants to do justice to sexual activity
must consider all these dimensions. This whole book could have
been devoted to the individual consideration of these characteristics of sexual activity. Do all these attributes have equal value?
Must they all be present when sexual intercourse is undertaken? Is
there a hierarchy of values? I have been preoccupied with these
questions a good deal of my life and I want to summarize my own
conclusions. These conclusions follow on from what I have
described so far.

I believe there is a hierarchy of values. The link between
instinct, person and love is so fundamental that it should be
pursued as an active priority whenever it is possible to do so. The
first link is between sex and love. In other words, the alienation
between the physical, the personal and love is the most fundamental disruption of sexuality.

Secondly, there is the link between sex and procreation.
Nature has imposed limitations on the woman in that fertility is
limited between puberty and the menopause. It is not a lifelong

characteristic. Again staying within the limits of physiology, the woman is fertile only for about twenty-four hours every month, suggesting very strongly that the loving component of sexual intercourse which is potentially present on each occasion has priority. But bringing children into the world is not primarily a matter of biology. Babies are persons and their numbers are dictated by psychosocial constraints. In some societies, children are essential as a pair of hands and as a support for old age. This is only partially true in the West, where in addition economic factors and women's emancipation have limited the size of the family drastically. So far, for all these reasons, the biological component is of secondary importance.

Thirdly, there is the accompanying pleasure of sexual activity. This is so powerful that the temptation to pursue it as an isolated outcome is very great. Clearly, from what has been said, the detachment of pleasure from personal interaction of love is an expression of human fragmentation.

Finally, there is the question of the comfort derived from the solitary pursuit of sexual activity in the course of which there is release from sexual tension. Here the minimum of the sexual potential is available but, as I shall show, it may be relevant on some occasions.

For me, sexual ethics depend on the sexual integrity of these four characteristics.

Masturbation

The pursuit of induced sexual pleasure with or without orgasm, usually solitary but sometimes mutually, frequently involving the genitals but sometimes involving other orifices of the body, is referred to as masturbation. I shall first deal with solitary masturbation.

As I said before, the Roman Catholic tradition of a generation ago was obsessed with masturbation, which was considered a grave or mortal sin. Indeed the pronouncement on Sexual Ethics in 1975 by the Holy Office still treats it as a grave sin. The reasons are classical. For the male it is an act which produces sexual pleasure and emission of semen outside the vagina and outside marriage, thus violating the link between sex and marriage and sex and procreation.

Returning to my own Roman Catholic tradition, I appreciate that, despite the orthodox teaching of the church, most moral theologians consider the commonest form of masturbation amongst adolescents as a much less serious moral violation. The reason given for this is the immaturity of the young and their lack of full knowledge and consent. In my writings I have claimed that it is no sin at all in adolescence. My reasons for this are as follows. If we pursue human development through its various phases, puberty with its hormonal changes in the body is a time when individuals are ready to acquaint themselves with their adult status. Masturbation is an essential part of this growth in self-awareness. It is primarily an experience of personal development and has no relationship to interpersonal love or procreation, and so neither of these issues of sexual integrity are involved.

Masturbation is next experienced in solitary situations such as prison or widowhood. Here personal growth does not apply. The individual is alone and uses masturbation for the relief of sexual tension and the realization of comfort, both minimal but essential characteristics of sexual activity. At the same time there is no violation of interpersonal love and procreation is not possible. Masturbation is also practised by the single person who is not in isolated situations. I believe the same principles as in solitary situations apply.

There is one other form of masturbation with different moral connotations. This is the masturbatory activity of husband or wife in the presence of each other's availability for heterosexual intercourse. In the course of my marital counselling I meet this problem regularly. Theoretically, the availability of husband and wife means that there is no need for masturbatory activity. Often masturbation is pursued because the spouse has been conditioned to this outlet from adolescence and the transfer to heterosexuality cannot be easily achieved. This matter is complex and needs a very careful individual assessment.

We turn now to mutual masturbation by adolescents, adults who
are homosexual and occasionally spouses. In all these situations
there is an interpersonal encounter and the criteria must be
whether love is present between the persons. For adolescents,
mutual masturbation is no more than sexual experimentation.
Homosexuals, as Bishop Montefiore has said, may indulge in
mutual masturbation as an expression of interpersonal affection
but without the possibility of procreation. Spouses may occasionally undertake mutual masturbation when there is a problem of
non-consummation, or difficulty with intercourse. While it is true
that procreative potential is missing, the presence or absence of
love is a powerful moral criterion of this behaviour.

Premarital Sexual Intercourse – Introduction

The overwhelming incidence of masturbation occurs in adolescence and is usually a transient phase on the way to sexual
intercourse. Bishop Montefiore is treating homosexuality, so I will
confine myself to heterosexual activity before marriage, an issue of
widespread interest nowadays when hardly any man or woman
enters marriage without some sexual experience.

The question whether young people should have sexual intercourse before marriage has apparently been settled by the fact that
they do so in practice. But does that conclude the matter? Is there
any enduring and universal reason why sexual intercourse should
be confined to marriage? Traditionally the reason given is that sex
is linked to procreation and that the fruit of this, children, need two
parents to look after them and give them legitimacy and status. The
matters of intercourse, pleasure and procreation within marriage
have been the enduring moral criteria. But as I have already said,
the link between sex and procreation has been most decidedly
broken by contraception. So why not pursue sex before and outside
marriage when procreation is deliberately excluded?

It will be appreciated by now that procreation is no longer the
primary criterion by which the morality of sexual intercourse is to
be assessed: in terms of the four criteria of love, procreation,
pleasure, relief of tension, the single most important is the

presence of love, which represents the highest unity of body and person. But what do we mean by love which is expressed by sexual intercourse?

Sexual love

For me sexual love is a body language in which a man and a woman are talking to each other with their bodies. They are communicating at least at six levels.

First and foremost every time they make love they are saying to each other, 'You are the most important person in my life. I want you. I appreciate you. I am enjoying your presence.' It is a moment which most profoundly confirms each other as persons. It is a recurrent affirmation of personhood.

Secondly, in the process of making love the man and the woman make available to each other not only their personhood but the totality of their sexuality. In and through intercourse the man makes the woman feel most completely feminine and the woman makes the man most completely masculine. It is a moment which confirms most completely each other's sexual identity. But it does something more. In the act the couple who are separate become one. This unity expresses the deepest sense of trusting availability.

Thirdly, most couples quarrel, fight and hurt each other. They quickly forget and forgive but sometimes the pain is deeper and more enduring. Then it needs something equivalently deep to take it away and that is to be found in sexual intercourse. So it can be an act of forgiveness and reconciliation.

Fourthly, every time we make love we are reinforced by the feeling of being wanted by somebody who matters in our life. It is a recurrent act of hope that we are still meaningful and needed.

Fifthly, the act gives us great pleasure and joy and we spontaneously want to give thanks to each other. It is a recurrent act of thanksgiving.

All these experiences apply to everybody, but there is a sixth dimension which is confined to Christians. The separation – unity, the dyad into one that intercourse produces – is a reminder of the Trinity in which three persons become one and still retain their separate identity. Sexual intercourse is an act of love in which the human and the divine meet and it is the central act of prayer in that couple's life.

All these meanings are potentially possible when the act occurs. But sexual intercourse influences interpersonal love as part of a wider relationship.

When a man and a woman relate they need to sustain each other as persons. This means they need to know and to be known. At the heart of sustaining is the wish to be known, understood and responded to accurately. We do this through empathy and appropriate communication, physically and emotionally. At the centre of sustaining is the moment of couple-communication through intercourse.

As we reveal ourselves to each other we discover not only our strengths but also our wounds. Every encounter between persons is an encounter between our intact and wounded selves. We come to each other feeling insecure and anticipating rejection, deprived, hungry for affection, lacking self-esteem and needing affirmation, short of confidence and needing reassurance, shy, confused and unsure of ourselves, at times moody, irritable and hurt. As we encounter each other we give the person we love a second chance to feel secure, wanted and appreciated. We tolerate his or her moods, fits of irritability and translate his or her longings for wholeness into reality. In other words, a loving relationship is concerned with healing. At the centre of healing is sexual intercourse which signals unconditional acceptance.

In the course of relating we change. We change our thoughts, attitudes, values, sense of confidence, initiative, priorities. We remain the same and yet we are constantly changing. Sexual intercourse, whilst always enacted with similar characteristics, is responding to an ever-changing person who is affirmed anew.

So sexual intercourse has a massive role to play in the sustaining, healing and facilitation of mutual growth. It is the one act that can constantly give life to the two people involved.

But if intercourse is to realize its potential, it needs to be carried out within the context of a continuing, reliable and predictable relationship. The full potential of sexual intercourse is to be seen as a source of life for two people who are relating over time. It is powerless to operate when it is experienced in transient, unreliable and unpredictable circumstances. The devaluation of sexual intercourse is to be found in transiency, impersonality and detachment.

The effective framework for sexual intercourse is a committed, permanent and faithful relationship and that is what marriage is. We are accustomed to think of marriage as a wedding ceremony. But marriage is essentially a committed relationship. The issue is not that sex is wrong before marriage and right after. The point is that sexual intercourse can only have justice done to its richness in a relationship we call marriage. Incidentally, the link between sexual intercourse and children is certainly biological, but infinitely more important is the contribution it makes to the stability of the spouses which gives the children the love and security which they need. Sexual intercourse is a main contributor to this stability, and this is its main significance for the life of the children. So at the heart of sexual love is the link between the physical and the personal in a committed relationship and it is against this background that premarital sexual intercourse has to be assessed.

Commitment

If commitment to an enduring, reliable and predictable relationship is the basis within which sexual intercourse belongs, then we can assess the morality of premarital sexual intercourse in terms of this criterion. I say this because at present all denominations consider premarital sexual intercourse as fornication. I would like to distinguish premarital sexual intercourse in terms of the loving commitment present.

The first pattern of sexual intercourse is between the client and the prostitute. Here every criterion I have mentioned is missing. The sexual act is set in an encounter which is casual, has no interpersonal exchange and no commitment. In these terms there is nothing that redeems the act. Yet prostitutes cater for a wide variety of men amongst whom are to be found the lonely, deprived, shy, handicapped, with a variety of unusual needs, in other words, some of the poorest human beings. I have no desire to idealize prostitution, but at the same time I cannot ignore the encounter between the poverty of the prostitute and that of her client. Objectively it is a severe impoverishment of sex, but only God can really know the emotional deprivation which encourages such encounters of comfort.

The second pattern is the one-night stand. This is set in the readiness and willingness to participate in sex in the course of a social gathering or in circumstances of social isolation with the object of having sexual pleasure. Once again, such casual sex meets none of its objective criteria of intergrity. Objectively it is not justifiable, but we have to be sensitive to the lonely, the isolated, those hungry for affection, those with inordinate desires who can only cope with casual and detached sex.

Moving from the casual and before we reach the point of sexual intercourse carried out during courtship, there is a variety of sexual activity in temporary, semi-committed relationships which are not casual, nor those of cohabitation. In these relationships, young people have a temporary sexual relationship which is acknowledged to serve sexual and emotional needs of the moment, but bears no commitment for the future. At the heart of sexual intercourse is the expression of love arising from a continuous, committed relationship. In so far as these conditions do not exist, these temporary relationships are in fact denying some of the essential features of sexuality. They are offering temporary security, and sexual outlets which are valid but subordinate sexual goals. They are also problematic. One partner may become more committed than the other, and when the relationship breaks up feels very distressed, used or exploited. In fact these relationships have a semblance of exploitation in which two people agree to use one another for sexual relief and temporary commitment before they are ready for permanent relationships. For me, sex is too precious and powerful a force to be used in this way.

Couples reach a stage when they are committed to each other and are waiting to get married. What is the status of sexual intercourse in this setting? Clearly most couples feel in these circumstances that they are already married and they have sexual intercourse. It is very difficult to find moral grounds for condemning this behaviour except that in fact couples can withdraw from marrying right up to the last minute and that a public ceremony seals a commitment in as full a human way as possible. But this is an ideal, and throughout history the moment of sexual intercourse has hovered from just before to just after the ceremony.

What I have tried to show in this section is that premarital sexual intercourse which can traditionally be called fornication is not a single entity, and it varies between the encounter of the prostitute and her client to intercourse in the few days before marriage. Clearly, the criterion of morality cannot be the same for all these occasions. The decisive shift, however, is the move away from looking at the biological criterion of procreation to the presence or absence of love.

Cohabitation

The final issue which must be tackled is cohabitation. This is a state in which a couple are living together as husband and wife. Cohabitation may be followed by formal marriage, but increasingly couples are deciding to cohabit, have children and not marry. What is the moral status of cohabitation?

In so far as such a couple have not undertaken a formal ceremony of marriage, they are in fact formally fornicating. However, they would not see themselves in that light at all. By the criteria I have set out, they are in fact in a state of committed love which is marriage. The concept that they are married without going through a formal ceremony is not a leap of the imagination or an externalizing liberal handout. There is a deep-seated theological tradition that the essence of marriage is to be found in the commitment and donation of a man and a woman of their person to each other in a committed relationship which is consummated by intercourse. It is not the priest who confers marriage. He is a witness to the marriage event which the couple enact for each other. The public dimension of the wedding ceremony was introduced as a compulsory element to safeguard that commitment.

I believe that the need for a public dimension of marriage is as relevant today as when it was introduced three hundred years ago. Nevertheless, the status of cohabitation is far from clear in the moral sense. Whilst such patterns of behaviour are clearly breaking ecclesiastical and legal laws, are they repudiating the essence of marriage?

Summary

Let me summarize what I have said in this chapter. For thousands of years the key to sexuality was to be found in procreation with the accompanying pleasure, a reward for this deed. The teaching on contraception in the Roman Catholic Church which insists that every act of intercourse should be open to life is the last remnant of this tradition. No one can dismiss the biological link between intercourse and new life, but the connection has become markedly reduced, and in my view a deeper understanding of the human personality shows that it is the link between sex and love that has the supreme value and that all intercourse has ultimately to be assessed by the presence or absence of love. The link between sex and love not only makes an authentic bridge between the secular and the Christian, giving everybody a criterion of sexual integrity which they can follow, but also brings sexual intercourse to the very heart of the mystery of the Godhead.

In the First Epistle of St John we are told that God is love, and in Genesis that man and woman were created in the image of God. It is no exaggeration to say that in sexual intercourse which is linked with love, couples are reflecting the most profound experience of God in their life.

God, Sex, Love

In the last twenty-five years, the permissive society has attempted to liberate sex from the confines of the furtive, the secretive, from shame and guilt. At the same time it has, at its worst, trivialized, cheapened and dehumanized it. Christianity has been shocked and its ethical foundations challenged. Crisis is a time of opportunity. Whilst we can thank the world as Christians for demystifying sex, we have an opportunity to offer back to the world a value of sexuality steeped in love which accords with the findings of psychology, the insights of the Bible and tradition, for sex has always been held in high regard. Today we can see it as a precious gift from God which demands a morality to protect not something we should feel embarrassed about but an experience that reflects the divine in each one of us.

3

Marriage and Marital Breakdown

Jack Dominian

The Judaeo-Christian tradition has regarded marriage basically as a secular reality taken up in the divine order. The concept of marriage had been present before the Jews received their mono-theistic revelation. But since then, marriage has been experienced as a gift from God to mankind. It is not my intention to trace the biblical roots of this topic and the ensuing theological development in the Christian tradition.[1] Suffice to say that in the Middle Ages the Western Church arrived at the notion of marriage as a sacrament which remains the teaching of the Roman Catholic Church to date. The Protestant tradition did not accept the sacramental state but acknowledged that marriage is a holy estate. Without spending too much time on the distinction between sacrament and holy estate, we must note the fact that there is a clear convergence in all Christian denominations on the view that the secular entity of marriage is transformed into a sacred reality. What I want to stress is that this sacred reality is intimately related to the underlying secular changes. If we are to understand the Christian mystery, we must first and foremost appreciate the unfolding human understanding of it. This is particularly pertinent today, when Western society is in the midst of major changes in its definition of matrimony.

What I would like to do in this chapter is to trace the

contemporary sociological and psychological changes of marriage
nd the response of the churches, and follow this up by examining
' implications of these changes for marital breakdown and the
al issues surrounding divorce.

The se   r reality of marriage

At the he.   of the changes following the Industrial Revolution is a
major separation between home and work. The predominant rural
world before that supported the husband and wife working
together on the land. Women worked as hard in the fields as the
men, but the family was not split up. The Industrial Revolution
was responsible for this shift of work outside the home. The factory
became the home for men during the day, and increasingly this
applied to women. The middle- and upper-class woman stayed at
home, and for the last hundred years the sociology of the family has
stressed the different functions of men and women at work and
home.

In the last thirty years these features have been selected for
notice by research workers. The first major issue is the change of
marriage from an institution primarily concerned with children to
a unit in which the chief feature is companionship between the
spouses and of the parents with their children. Within this
framework of companionship, the American sociologist Talcott
Parsons stressed the structure of marriage in terms of fixed
conjugal roles.[2] Thus the husband was the person who heads the
family, takes the important decisions and is the economic provider.
The wife is the childbearer and rearer and the source of affection
for the family. Generations of people have grown up with this
image of marriage: provided the couples carry out these duties, the
marriage is then considered successful.

This view of marriage was criticized as being too rigid and static,
so in due course the notion developed that marriage is symmetrical,
the word used by Young and Willmott[3] to indicate an internal
world in which the spouses relate on an egalitarian basis, with
authority and functions shared and exchanged. This symmetrical

type of marriage has other features as well. It is influenced by woman's emancipation, with increasing emphasis on her work and, even more important, greater expectations of a more loving marital relationship. Thus, for many people today, marriage is expected to be egalitarian, with high expectations of fulfilment, emotionally and sexually, a relationship in which love plays a crucial role in the viability of the relationship.

Finally and imperceptibly, there have been the changes in the Divorce Law which in subtle but major ways affect our understanding of marriage. The Divorce Act of 1971 in England and Wales, later to be followed in Scotland, made irretrievable breakdown the sole ground for divorce in Britain. Few people appreciate what a radical change this has been in our understanding of marriage. Prior to this change in the law, the essential understanding of marriage was its contractual basis. At the moment of marriage the man and the woman entered into a contract of an exclusive lifelong commitment and mutual fidelity. When desertion, cruelty and adultery took place, these were considered offences against the contract. Now the same patterns of behaviour are considered as an unacceptable basis for marital life and the emphasis is no longer on the violation of a contract but on the viability of a relationship.

There is thus a convergence between theoretical models and the law, showing that marriage is changing from a contract to a relationship, with the inner world of marriage seeking egalitarian exchanges between the sexes, emphasizing fulfilment in affection and sex, all united under an umbrella of love.

The Christian response

How have the Christian churches responded to these secular changes? I start with the statement from the Roman Catholic Church in the Second Vatican Council, not because I want to give that church any precedence but in order to show the transformation in that denomination from a totally legalistic interpretation of marriage, in which Canon Law was its inspiration,

to a biblical understanding which has appreciated the secular
changes.

In the Second Vatican Council the familiar language of centuries
in terms of primary and secondary ends of marriage was dropped.
Instead, marriage and the family were called 'a community of love'.
Marriage is now regarded as a 'conjugal covenant'. The following
statement sums up the teaching: 'Hence, by that human act
whereby spouses mutually bestow and accept each other, a
relationship arises which by divine will and in the eyes of society
too is a lasting one'.[4] The emphasis is now on love, relationship and
covenant, all integrated into a dynamic community.

The Church of England has produced two reports on marriage,
in 1971 and 1978.[5] In the second report the authors, contrasting the
purposes of marriage in terms of children and the conjugal life of
the spouses, state: 'We, on the other hand, wish to affirm that
marriage is best understood as "for" husband and wife. It is their
relationship with each other which is the basis for marriage. On
this is built their relationship with their children.'[6]

The report on Personal Relationship to the General Assembly of
the Church of Scotland in 1970 had this to say on Christian
marriage: 'Christian marriage is to be seen primarily as a relationship with God, in which a man and a woman, in love and respect for
each other, are utterly committed to each other, in an equal
partnership in all things until death do them part.'

Other denominations have responded in a similar way. We can
thus see that in the last twenty-five years major changes have
shifted our understanding of marriage from contract to a relationship of love. It is a shift which Christianity has accepted totally, and
indeed it would be surprising if it had not, for the concept of
marriage as a relationship based on love is consistent with the
deepest elements of the Christian faith.

I should say at once that one of the consequences of this change
has been widespread marital breakdown in Western Society. From
the Christian point of view, we have the paradox that a major
change in the understanding and practice of marriage as a
relationship of love has led to a consequence which is entirely in

disagreement with the Christian tradition of indissolubility. How is this paradox to be explained? I believe that rapidly rising expectations of women's rights, and deeper fulfilment in the personal relationship of love and sex, came with such rapidity that there was no time to prepare and support modern marriage for these ideals. From the Christian point of view, something even more sinister has occurred. The areas where the changes are taking place such as woman's status, sexual fulfilment and the psychological understanding of intimacy are notoriously areas where Christianity is weak and has ignored, for example, a great deal of the advances of a century of psychology. For me the greatest scandal has been that a faith based on love has not been able to take the initiative to inspire people with the meaning of love in their marriage life. The failure of the church to respond creatively to the modern understanding of marriage in terms of love and sexuality is one of the major reasons for the large-scale withdrawal of people from the institutional churches which we are witnessing in so much of the Western world. The two major experiences of human beings are work and love, and the latter is expressed primarily in marriage. The conspicuous absence of a major contribution from Christianity to either is one of its major weaknesses, and I consider the Christian response to marriage one of the main ethical issues of our age, which transcends the usual questions of sexual ethics that are normally hotly debated.

My own writings of the last twenty years have returned repeatedly to an attempt to understand marital love in terms of the unfolding notion of contemporary marriage. In my book *Marriage, Faith and Love* I tried to summarize my main ideas on love expressed in the personal relationship of the spouses.

In that book I described two phases of marital love. The first is the state of falling in love, which is present in courtship and the early years of marriage. In this phase the couple are consumed with an idealized awareness of each other. They find each other's body and personality overwhelming and want to communicate as much as possible with each other. Conflict is easily forgiven and forgotten. Positive aspects are noted and exaggerated and negative ones dismissed and minimized. It is a pleasure to be in each other's company and mutual presence renews life. This phase of being in love, research tells us, begins to diminish from the first day of marriage! But it continues for some time, to be gradually replaced by loving. In the intimacy of contemporary marriage, loving means returning to the key experiences of our first relationship of love between ourselves and our parents in childhood. In this exchange such experiences as attachment, trust, intimacy and autonomy, conflict and forgiveness, authenticity versus superficiality, availability versus egoism, empathy versus alienation, communication versus withdrawal, gentleness versus aggression, are the ingredients out of which love is constructed. In our married life we do not ordinarily compile such a list and tick off relevant happenings at the end of each day. It is research workers who construct such lists, manipulate the figures statistically and come up with a version of love which is incomprehensible to everyone but keeps sociologists and psychologists happy as they acquire this material for the next PhD thesis.

Love needs to be translated into easily recognizable categories of needs met by our partner. With this in mind, I have described three central experiences of loving in all personal relationships, but particularly in marriage, sustaining, healing and growth.

The symbol of sustaining is a cup containing wine. The cup is the outward supportive framework of the couple which provides money to finance everyday life, a house for living and work with its wide-ranging implications. When people talk about the problems facing modern marriage they often refer to these material aspects of sustaining. But there is overwhelming evidence that, even when the material sustaining is ample, marriages can run into difficulties. We then need to look at the wine in the cup, which constitutes the inner world of the personal relationship of the couple. By sustaining here I mean the level of communication, the expression of feelings of affection and the sensitive awareness of each other as a person. Women are very much better communicators than men. Regretfully men call women's communication nagging. Often when the man comes from work and his wife asks him what happened during the day, he thinks seriously about it and produces the laconic reply, 'Nothing, dear'. When it comes to expressing affection, once again women are much better at saying 'I love you' in a multitude of ways. I meet couples repeatedly where the husband says 'I told you I love you twenty-five years ago, why do you want to hear it again? I'm still here, isn't that enough?' The sensitive awareness of each other is crucial for sustaining love. We all want to be known and understood, preferably as we were when we were children, when parents knew magically what we needed. Growing up does not remove our need for being recognized, wanted, appreciated sensitively by each other. Yet once again women are so much better at awareness than men. Men often find women a mystery and rationalize their lack of comprehension by indicting them as irrational, and when that doesn't work, they blame the monthly period or the menopause for everything that happens to women. Some men seem to think the menopause starts at twenty! One of the reasons for the widespread incidence of divorce is that women have greater expectations of these internal levels of sustaining and are not prepared to put up with instances of gross insensitivity.

We come next to healing. All of us are wounded people. Physical wounds are most clearly visible; emotional ones are more ubiquitous and hidden. These wounds are created from the combined impact of our genetic make-up and our parental experiences. As a psychiatrist I have spent the last thirty years responding to the ten per cent of society who are most wounded. But all of us suffer to a greater or lesser extent from feelings of anxiety, depression, moodiness, moments of peak aggression, hostility, suspicion, mistrust, lack of confidence, lack of self-esteem, feelings of emotional deprivation, fears of being abandoned, pessimism, lack of initiative and many other negative characteristics. When we come to marriage, we long for understanding of our wounds and for a second opportunity to repair the damage. We want our spouse to heal us by giving us encouragement, reassurance, security, confidence and appreciation. The enormous preoccupation with sex in our society suggests that the only peak moment in marriage is when we are making love. I have no desire to minimize that particular peak, but in fact the same can be achieved in a series of momentary peaks as we are rescued from our gloom and doom, the sense of despair, reassured that we have meaning and purpose in life, that we are successful and effective despite our lack of self-esteem. When couples are so wounded that their mutual needs exceed their emotional resources the marriage cannot survive. But in the majority of marriages there is a complementarity of resources, and couples donate to each other the confidence, trust and security which not only can help them to overcome in some instances alcoholism, drug abuse and gambling, but in the majority of cases also slowly transform and heal the personality. Marriage is probably the single most important source of healing in society. Once again, when the partner is too insensitive to respond to one's needs, the temptation nowadays is to look elsewhere for a more accommodating partner. I cannot leave healing without remarking that it is at the centre of our faith as we all try slowly and painfully to be Christ-like. Christianity chooses to make forgiveness its key human contribution to healing, but forgiveness without change in our personality is a sterile experience if we neither learn nor change. If forgiveness is to be effective, it needs *metanoia*, a change of heart, and psychology has taught us more about the mechanisms of change than any other science. Spouses are involved daily in these processes of change and can either alienate and confirm each other in their wounds or give them the experiences and opportunities to change. The psychoanalyst has become the guru of the twentieth century, but we know from research that all the mechanisms of transfrence, countertransference, coping with phantasy and reality, aggression and love, which the analyst treats as his tools for effecting change, take place all the time in the intimacy of marriage, and the healing that is effected in psychoanalysis occurs in a much slower and less focussed way in marriage. An enormous amount of work needs to be done to translate the skills of psychodynamic therapy into everyday transactions of spouses. It is occurring all the time, but we have to help people appreciate clearly these moments.

The third dimension of love involves change. There are many who assert that as modern marriage covers a span of some fifty years, it is impossible to live with the same partner for all this time. The key to this challenge is to appreciate that we change over time. We change in our appearance, thus putting sexual attraction at risk; we change in our ideas, values and priorities, risking alienation; we change our needs, making the partner we chose at twenty irrelevant at forty. These are the risks, and the first step of prevention is to become familiar with these patterns of changes. There are also advantages. It is an enormous benefit to be accompanied over fifty years by someone who travels by your side and both appreciates and facilitates your changes, assisting you to realize your potential, to become creative, one who supports you when you fall, helps you when you become sick, all the time understanding and appreciating each successive layer of your being which uncovers the balance between the majesty and poverty of your personality. To be accompanied by the same person is portrayed as boring, but it is infinitely more difficult to start from scratch with a new person every time you want to write another chapter of your life. Reliable continuity rather than a restless change is the key to growth. The three persons in the Trinity do not get bored with each other because their life substance is the fullness of love. In my three key concepts of sustaining, healing and growth, I have identified some of the precursors of that fullness of love. I have no doubt there are many others and many alternative variations in describing loving. But my dream is that as the secular world of marriage and the Christian response converge on the reality of love, Christianity may seek the best of its own tradition, couple it with the best from the social sciences and begin to give men and women not only an outline of the goal of love, but the translation into concrete loving experiences which match the yearnings of people.

I consider the convergence of secular and Christian marriage in love to be a unique opportunity for Christianity to offer a profound understanding of the inner world of marriage and to help people realize their expectations through widespread programmes of

marital preparation, support for marriage and marriage enrich-
ment. We have a golden opportunity to translate the notion that
God is love into a practical application that will meet the secular
needs of the married. At the Second Vatican Council the Roman
Catholic Church coined the phrase 'the domestic church'. By this
it means that married life, steeped in the love I have outlined, with
its successes and its failures, is one of the most potent encounters
with God. The married have their own church at home which is as
powerful a meeting point with the Lord as actually going to the
building of the church. For me this is an extremely fruitful idea,
full of evangelization potential. I would like to see our century be
the beginning of a real spiritual and theological shift whereby the
home becomes as powerful a spiritual community as the fellowship
of the local church. And in case anybody thinks that the picture I
have presented is too inward looking, let me say at once that a
secure and loving marriage is the background from which we are
most likely to go out and meet and love our neighbour. If our
marriage is in distress, a good deal of our energy is taken up with
survival and we have very little time for anybody else except to
prop us up.

Marital breakdown

That is the dream. Now we have to deal with the reality of marital
breakdown and divorce. I have already presented my main thesis
why there has been such a massive escalation of divorce in most
Western countries since 1960.[7] The reason is that the inner world
of marriage, particularly on the part of women, has changed with
the rapid rise of expectations, some of which I have outlined, with
the absence of a concomitant education and support for these
changes.

I am not going to blind you with statistics. Sufficient to say that
there has been a 600% increase in divorce in the last twenty-five
years in Britain. In 1961, there were 25,000 divorces in England
and Wales and 2,000 in Scotland. In 1983, the numbers had
increased to 150,000 and 13,000 respectively. In Britain as a whole,
some half a million men, women and children leave the divorce

courts every year. It is calculated that one in three marriages in Britain are heading for dissolution.[8] The figure in the USA is one in two. Although divorce figures have stabilized in the last five years, the present plateau is extremely high, and I consider divorce to be the single most important social and moral issue of our day.

The consequences are massive. No one visualizes the complete picture. The doctor sees the stress symptoms associated with marital conflict; the hospital the consequences in alcohol consumption, affective disorders, suicidal attempts, suicides and general disease. The teacher sees the adverse consequences on children in their behaviour at school; the clergy the immense moral dilemmas posed by divorce; the magistrate the results of juvenile delinquency; the solicitor the unhappiness and anger of frustrated spouses; and society picks up the bill of nearly two billion pounds a year as a cost of marital breakdown. I have briefly referred to the adverse effects on spouses,[9] but recent research has highlighted how damaging divorce is for children,[10] including the fact that divorce children have a higher chance of ending their own marriages in divorce.

I believe that the damage of divorce is immense, and that no one, including the churches, has appreciated the cost of our divorce-habituated society. Second marriages are even riskier entities than first marriages, and although some second marriages are very happy for the adults, the cost to the children is very great.

I mention all this because I want to place the ethical issues in perspective. The churches have been preoccupied with the moral dilemmas of remarriage after divorce. But for me, the major issue is divorce itself. Society and the church have been concerned with picking up the pieces after divorce in such matters as remarriage in church, legislation for the needs of the divorced and the care of their children. All this is important. But the most important issue is the prevention of divorce, and about this only too little has been said and done. It was for this reason that I set up the Marriage Research Centre in 1971 at my hospital, the Central Middlesex Hospital in London, whose main purpose is research-orientated prevention work.

Ethical issues of divorce

Returning to the ethical issues that have concerned the churches in matters concerning divorce, they are essentially two. The first is the concept of divorce itself. Can a couple who are in a Christian marriage obtain a divorce? Secondly, if they are divorced, can they be remarried in church?

The answer to the first question, namely that of divorce itself, varies amongst the churches. Thus the Roman Catholic Church believes that a marriage properly entered into and consummated by sexual intercourse which becomes a sacrament cannot be dissolved. The Orthodox Churches allow more than one divorce. The Protestant tradition of Luther and Calvin admits divorce on the grounds of adultery and desertion. The various churches base their conclusions on the different interpretations of Matthew's exemption clause and Paul's teaching in Corinthians. We can see that the Roman Catholic Church has, in theory, the strictest tradition. In practice, it has a widespread network for grounds of nullity assessed by the church tribunals which were abolished at the time of the Reformation but which have remained in operation in the Roman Catholic Church. Many are suspicious of these tribunals and their grounds for annulment, which basically assume that, despite many years of marriage, the marriage has never properly existed, and in the eyes of many this makes the whole process a mockery.

The new Canon Law[11] specifies clearly that matrimonial consent was not validly given if it can be shown that at the time of the marriage one partner or both suffered from a grave lack of discretionary judgment concerning the essential matrimonial rights and obligations to be undertaken in marriage. Matrimonial consent is also not present because of causes of a psychological nature which impede the person from assuming the essential obligations of marriage. These two grounds have become widely known as a basis for nullity.

In my view none of these approaches is entirely satisfactory. The Orthodox and Protestant traditions admit of divorce, and the Roman Catholic one, whilst denying divorce officially, allows for cases of annulment.

Nevertheless, the Christian position is clear. Whilst the Old Testament permitted divorce, the ideal was permanency. Jesus is clearly against divorce in the most forceful language, and that must be concluded to be the mind of God. However, marriages do break down: that is the human predicament, and the church from the time of Matthew and Paul has made allowances for that fact. My own position is that we have overwhelming evidence from secular research that divorce is damaging to spouses and children and that in this ethical matter, science and Christianity are in one accord about the goal for which we should be striving. My conclusion is that we should spend infinitely less time with the theological texts and inject far more resources into the research and understanding of marital breakdown. The church must be seen to put its money where its heart is. The Marriage Research Centre, which receives no grant from the British government urgently needs a big injection of money to carry out its task of research on prevention.

As far as the theological understanding of divorce is concerned, I take the view that the best Christian answer is to back research on patterns of marital conflict so that we can understand when the minimum conditions for marriage exist and where no such conditions are possible. It is no use defending the indefensible. If two people cannot undertake the marital relationship, then no marriage exists, however long they may have been living as husband and wife. This is why I prefer the Roman Catholic system, which tries to lay down minimum conditions of what a marriage is and safeguards these. It is the only system, however imperfect, which attempts to remain true to the values of Jesus whilst recognizing that some couples cannot undertake the obligations of marriage. The Orthodox and Protestant positions have the advantage of simplicity, but do not help us to distinguish between what can be saved from that which is humanly impossible. The ultimate ideal is to recognize through research patterns of marital difficulties which can be overcome, giving the couple at least a minimum of marital fulfilment. These situations ought to be identifiable and given maximum support. Patterns that cannot work at all should also be identified and discouraged *ab initio*, or if entered into should be open to release. My reasoning is that the inner world of marriage, however complicated, is not a complete mystery, and careful research should help both society and religion to protect and save what can be saved whilst recognizing that, in some instances, a couple cannot succeed. The overall ethical answer is less abstruse theological debates and more active understanding.

Conclusion

I will finish by reasserting that we are in the midst of a major revolution in marriage which emphasizes the conjugal unity as a personal relationship of egalitarian and loving proportions. Recent research such as our latest book from the Marriage Research Centre[12] affirms that the egalitarian reality is far from complete. Women are still largely expected to work, look after the home and raise the children. But men are understanding much more. There is a paradox that the movement towards a more loving personal relationship has been accompanied by massive divorce. I believe that the time is opportune for the churches to enter the field of marriage in a major way and make love the bridge between the secular and the Christian. Marriage has waited for a long time for a major theological and spiritual thrust, and the time is now opportune to encourage this development. For this to happen we need a major theological revolution in which we reappraise the wedding not as the point where the church concludes its dealings with the married but rather where it begins a long journey of accompanying them over the next fifty years with support and encouragement. At the same time we need to develop a theology that makes the home, marriage and the family a central focus of the spiritual experience of its members, so that the church in the future will see the twentieth century as the beginning of a new spirituality for the lay person.

4

Homosexuality

Hugh Montefiore

My subject is homosexuality. Let me define my terms. A homosexual is a man or a woman who is sexually attracted to a person of the same sex. The word should refer to someone with this kind of orientation, but it is often, in common parlance, used to refer to someone who engages in homosexual practice. Let me say that I do not use it in that sense in this chapter unless I specifically refer to sexual activity. I should also mention that because of the limited space available here I shall be confining myself to a discussion of male homosexuality.

I would also like at the outset to distinguish homosexuality from the very different conditions known as paedophilia and pederasty. Homosexuality concerns sexual attraction between adults, similar to that between heterosexuals except that the two people concerned belong to the same sex. Paedophilia concerns sex directed towards young children. Pederasty concerns sex directed towards boys around the age of puberty. In so far as both the latter are concerned with young people under the age of consent, both constitute criminal sexual abuse.

Homosexuality is an explosive subject for many reasons. Homosexuals often feel, not without justification, that they are unfairly treated in the society and culture in which they are living. They may well be the objects of discrimination and censure by others, so that they feel isolated and condemned. A few of them react by becoming increasingly strident and by insisting that their unions are on a par with heterosexual marriage. Most homosexuals, however, react very differently: they regret their sexual orientation, and they are too frightened to disclose it even to their family and friends. The condition of those who despise and even persecute them has actually been given a name: homophobia, fear of homosexuals.

Why so many people feel a hatred of the homosexual condition is a difficult matter to explain. There are those who say that such people are fighting suppressed homosexual tendencies in themselves. Others insist that they are naturally opposed to tendencies and practices which are in themselves unnatural. Most, I suspect, are the victims of a long-established cultural prejudice.

Although homosexuality is very uncommon in African cultures, there are a good number of homosexuals in Western society. The Kinsey Report on the *Sexual Behaviour of the Human Male* was published forty years ago. The conclusion drawn from its investigations was that 5% of white Western males and females have a predominantly homosexual orientation: that is to say, one in twenty persons. This conclusion was anticipated by Havelock Ellis fifty years earlier; and so it is likely to be still valid fifty years later as well. According to Kinsey, among a large and carefully checked group of white Americans, 37% had had some overt homosexual experience between adolescence and old age, while 8% of the males were exclusively homosexual for a period of three years between the ages of sixteen and fifty-five. Among women, some 13% had had explicitly Lesbian experience by the age of forty-five.

This evidence confirmed that some people have an exclusive homosexual orientation, others have been predominantly homosexual for a period of their lives, and others are in varying degrees bisexual, attracted to either sex. Opinions have differed about why this happens. Partly it may be due to circumstances. Prisoners, for example, are more likely than others to engage in homosexual activity during the period of their constraint, but they usually return to heterosexual activity after their release. Similarly boys in single-sex residential schools may well have some homosexual experience during their schooldays, although the majority grow up to become heterosexual men. Some children and boys, subjected to sexual abuse when young, may suffer later as a result, and one effect may be homosexual behaviour. Some people who find themselves bisexual make a definite choice to be homosexual. But the fact is that no one knows why a person has a homosexual orientation from an early age. Gender stereotyping is learnt by very young children, but there is little evidence that homosexuality arises from a confusion of this kind. Others speak of the influence of a dominant mother; but many people with very dominant mothers are heterosexuals. Others have supposed that the condition is due to a disturbed family situation. By the nature of the case, it would be unusual for homosexuality to be inherited. The condition could be due to some foetal abnormality; but many think that it is caused by some genetic mutation which creates a hormonal imbalance. The truth is that we simply do not know.

Is the condition permanent? That depends on the individual concerned. For those born with a strong homosexual orientation, the condition seems unalterable. Various therapies have been suggested: psychological, physical or spiritual; none has been shown to be universally effective. In fact, two types of homosexuality have been distinguished, both with what I regard as rather objectionable names: perverts and inverts. Perverts are those who need not be homosexuals; inverts are those who cannot alter their condition. This chapter is conerned only with inverts.

It is only in the recent past that church people have shown much Christian compassion and love towards those who find themselves with a homosexual orientation. At present members of mainstream churches are divided on the morality of homosexual practice, but their official positions are unanimously opposed to it. The situation has hardly been helped by the spread of AIDS in Western Countries, mainly among sexually active homosexuals.

First let us consider the official position of the churches. The Roman Catholic Church, in a statement on sexual ethics published in 1976 by the Congregation of the Faith, concluded that homosexual acts are 'intrinsically disordered, and can in no case be approved of';[1] at the same time, 'homosexuals must certainly be treated with understanding . . . their culpability will be judged with prudence.'[2] Ten years later, a letter to bishops of the Roman Catholic Church was published by the same source, this time on the pastoral care of homosexual persons. The position was reaffirmed, but a warning was added:

> In the discussion which followed the publication of the Declaration, an overly benign interpretation was given to the homosexual condition itself, some going so far as to call it neutral, or even good. Although the particular inclination of the homosexual person is not a sin, it is a more or less strong tendency ordered towards an intrinsic moral evil; and thus the inclination itself must be seen as an objective disorder.[3]

The Church of England's position is not so clear-cut. A report, published in 1979, and commissioned by its Board for Social Responsibility (although the Board itself felt unable to endorse it), reached the following conclusions:

> We do not think it possible to deny that there are circumstances in which individuals may justifiably choose to enter into a homosexual relationship with the hope of enjoying a companionship and physical expression of sexual love similar to that which is to be found in marriage.[4]

In 1983 the General Assembly of the Church of Scotland commended a report in which all homosexual acts were condemned, as they are also in the Episcopal Church in the USA.

In a debate of the General Synod of the Church of England in 1981, Dr Runcie, Archbishop of Canterbury, spoke of the homosexual condition 'not as a sin or as a sickness but more as a handicap.'[5] At first sight this may seem derogatory, but nowadays we tend to treat the handicapped not with contempt but with admiration. In 1981 the General Synod did not press the matter to a conclusion, but it returned to the matter in 1987 when it resolved that homosexual genital acts 'fall short of an ideal'. In contrast to fornication and adultery, homosexual genital acts were not explicitly called sinful, but at the same time they merit 'a call to repentance'. In the following year the 1988 Lambeth Conference resolved that all sexual genital acts should be confined to marriage.

So far as I know, no mainstream church – certainly in England – has officially approved of homosexual practice. Nonetheless, among Anglican churches the debate has not yet been concluded. The Episcopal Church of the USA determined in 1979 that celibacy and faithful monogamous marriage were the only two options open to Christians. In 1988 this limiting option was removed, but nothing was put in its place. In 1988 a book was published by Bishop John Spong of Newark, New Jersey, which included a vigorous defence of homosexual practice against 'the everpresent prejudice born out of a pervasive ignorance which attacks people who are born with an unchangeable predisposition towards those of their own sex'.[7] Meanwhile in England the Board for Social Responsibility had set up a new Commission to review the situation, and its report on the subject has been submitted to the House of Bishops, although its contents are as yet unknown.

Any Christian examination of the subject will begin with a consideration of the scriptural evidence. The Vatican Declaration on Sexual Ethics notes that, so far as homosexual acts are concerned, 'in Sacred Scripture they are condemned as a serious depravity, and even presented as the sad consequence of rejecting God.' Evangelicals base their objections to homosexual practice wholly on the evidence of the scriptures. We must ask ourselves what we ourselves make of these passages.

The best known is the story of Sodom and Gomorrah (Gen. 19. 1–26). Two angels came to Sodom, and Lot, Abraham's nephew who was living there, offered them hospitality overnight. But the citizens of Sodom came and demanded the two men, as they said, 'that we may known them'. Lot refused, and offered them instead his two virgin daughters. But the crowd threatened Lot with violence and it was with difficulty that he locked out the crowd; and in the morning the two angels persuaded him and his wife and his two unmarried daughters to flee before fire and brimstone destroyed the cities of the plain.

Interestingly enough, when Sodom and Gomorrah are mentioned elsewhere in the scriptures, it is not in connection with homosexuality. In Isaiah the people of Sodom and Gomorrah are convicted of insincere worship and injustice and oppression (Isa. 1. 10–20); in Jeremiah, it is adultery and lying (Jer. 23. 14); according to Ezekiel, 'This was the iniquity of your sister Sodom; she and her daughters had pride of wealth and food in plenty, comfort and ease, and yet she never helped the poor and the wretched. They grew haughty and did deeds abominable in my sight' (Ezek. 16. 49). According to Ecclesiasticus, it was because of their arrogance that the Sodomites were abhorred (Ecclus. 16. 8), while in the Wisdom of Solomon it was their lack of hospitality (19. 13f.). Elsewhere in the Old Testament and Apocrypha Sodom was regarded as a sink of iniquity from which came all manner of evil, rather than associated with homosexual practice; and the same may be said of the New Testament references, except just possibly for the Epistle of Jude (v. 7).

In the light of this, it has been suggested that in the Genesis story the men of Sodom simply wanted to know who Lot's visitors were.[9] They needed to assure themselves that the intention behind the strangers' visit was not malign; and Lot resisted their request because of the sacred laws of hospitality, which made it preferable for him to sacrifice his daughters to their lust rather than to subject his visitors to such inquisition. Certainly the words 'that we may know them' can be understood in their normal meaning rather than with a sexual connotation in the sense of 'carnal knowledge'. Yet only three verses on, Lot uses the same word of his own daughters with an evidently sexual connotation: 'I have two daughters which have not known man.' It is unlikely that the same word would be used three verses later with a very different meaning. It would have been quite consonant with the evil habits of the Sodomites to humiliate suspected strangers by a kind of gang buggery.

Similar to this story from Genesis is an equally unsavoury passage in the Book of Judges, so similar that some critics have

wondered whether it has not been derived from it. In this story
(Judges 19. 22–25), a Levite from the hill-country of Ephraim with
his concubine and her servant pass the night with an old man at
Gibeah, in Benjaminite territory. Like Lot at Sodom, the old man
is not a native of the area. As at Sodom, some scoundrels demand
that the Levite be brought out to them – and here the same word is
used: 'that we may know him'. The host offers instead his virgin
daughter for them to ravish. When the men refused this offer, the
Levite gave them instead his concubine, who died as a result,
thereby causing a tribal war between Benjamin and the other
tribes. The story has the same ambiguities as the Sodom story, so
that it could be simply a story about the resistance of a host against
the maltreatment of a foreigner who was a guest in his house. Since
it is likely that this story is connected in some way with the Sodom
story, the interpretation of the word to 'know' is likely to be the
same in both tales.

There are several references in the scriptures to the attempt to
eradicate the cult of sacred prostitution first in the hill shrines of
Canaan and then later at Jerusalem. It would be wrong, however,
to attach too much importance to these, because it is not clear
that the phrase 'male prostitute' necessarily implies homosexual
activity. More relevant are texts in Leviticus. In Leviticus 18, the
prohibition on homosexual practice is coupled with a prohibition
against bestialism in a list of forbidden sexual relationships. In a
second list of sexual offences in Leviticus 20, we read:

If a man has intercourse with a man as with a woman, they both
commit an abomination. They shall both be put to death: their
blood shall be on their own heads (Lev. 20. 13).

'Abomination' has a cultic overtone, and this is a prohibition of
cultic prostitution along with other Canaanite cultic practices.
But there is also implicit in the use of the Hebrew word for
'abomination' the idea of unnatural intercourse. Men were created
to have intercourse with women, not with other men or with
beasts.

It is possible to adopt either a minimizing or a maximizing

attitude to the Old Testament evidence. Either one can say that the
Sodom and Gibeah stories are not about homosexuality, but about
hospitality, and that the other references concern homosexual
practice as a form of cultic prostitution in order to ensure fertility
which is condemned so strongly because Israel was ordered to
separate itself from pagan practice. Or one can say that the Sodom
story is indeed about homosexuality, and that it shows the
judgment of God on such practices, and that the references in the
Jewish law, while they may be concerned with cultic prostitution,
show a true and enduring insight into sexual ethics, based in part
on primitive insight into natural law.

When we turn to the New Testament, we find nothing reported
on the lips of Jesus about homosexuality. He is reported more than
once to have mentioned Sodom and Gomorrah, but only to show
that lack of faith and repentance will bring a fate worse than that of
the inhabitants of the cities of the plain. Whatever they were or were
not guilty of, there would be worse penalties for other offences.

St Paul condemns homosexuality in strong terms in three
passages. The first and longest of these is to be found in his Epistle
to the Romans, which comes closer than any other of his extant
writings to a systematic exposition of his understanding of
Christian belief and practice. In his first chapter Paul describes the
godless world. Men and women can know God, and indeed they
do, but they refuse to honour him. As a result they flounder in the
vileness of their own desires and degrade their bodies, worshipping
the creature rather than the Creator. Their lives are characterized
by idolatry and immorality. Paul continues:

> In consequence, I say, God has given them up to shameless
> passions. Their women have exchanged natural intercourse for
> unnatural, and their men in turn, giving up natural relations
> with women, burn with lust for one another; males behave
> indecently with males and are paid in their own persons the
> fitting wage of such perversion (Rom. 1. 26–7).

Paul then goes on to describe the total moral chaos of the pagan
world, giving a terrible list of evil and immorality, ending with the

affirmation that such people 'are without natural affection and without pity' (v. 31). (Some exegetes have suggested that, so far as women are concerned, Paul is not referring to Lesbianism, but to what might have seemed to Jews as unnatural practices of heterosexual intercourse.) The male reference here is clearly to homosexual practice, and Paul regarded this as wrong because it offended against the natural law which God had written into human sexuality. In this passage in Romans Paul is referring to a state of moral chaos where 'anything goes'. Among all the evils of pagan life in the Roman Empire nothing filled contemporary Jews in the Hellenistic world with greater contempt than the widespread practices of pederasty and homosexuality. Paul's description here is utterly removed from that of a permanent and faithful relationship between two homosexual people who are united to each other by enduring ties of love and affection. He does not seem to have in mind people with a permanent homosexual orientation, but rather those who had had heterosexual relations but who have given them up for homosexual lust; in other words, bisexuals who opted for the homosexual alternative, living lives of extravagant promiscuity.

In Paul's first letter to the Corinthians, written earlier than that to the Romans, Paul is warning his readers against falling back into their pagan ways in a city notorious for its sexual immorality:

> Surely you know that the unjust will never come into the possession of the Kingdom of God. Make no mistake; no fornicator, or idolater, none who are guilty either of adultery or of sexual perversion, no thieves or grabbers or drunkards or slanderers or swindlers will possess the Kingdom of God. Such were some of you (I Cor. 6. 9–10).

The phrase rendered in NEB 'guilty of sexual perversion' translates two words in Greek. The first, *malakoi*, means 'softies' and refers to males who play a passive role in intercourse, while the second word, *arsenokoitai*, means 'those who lie with men' and refers to a pederast or active homosexual. Once again, Paul seems not to be referring to love, but rather to lust, both heterosexual and homosexual, amid the general state of immorality in the pagan

Hellenistic world, as a reason for exclusion from the Kingdom of God.

In the third passage Paul, or whoever wrote the First Epistle to Timothy, is explaining that the law is aimed not at good citizens but at the bad (I Tim. 1.8–11). There then occurs a list of people who need the restraint of law, among whom are listed homosexuals – the word used is *arsenokoitai* – sandwiched between murderers and fornicators on the one hand, and kidnappers and liars on the other. Once again, Paul seems to be referring to occasions of lust, not of love.

I do not suppose that Paul would have distinguished between homosexual orientation and homosexual practice: such a distinction was alien to the culture in which he lived. It clearly did not enter Paul's head that there could be such a thing as genuine homosexual love between two adults: he thought of homosexuality as an exercise of lust and debauchery. He also saw it as a manifestation of evil in a pagan world which had turned its back upon the one true God.

But I do not think that Paul simply restated the Jewish tabu on homosexual relations: it seems to me that he had thought the matter out afresh in the light of Christ's teaching on sex, which he repeated in the Epistle to the Ephesians (Eph. 5.31). Jesus, as recounted in all three Synoptic Gospels (Mark 10. 2–12 *et al.*), responded to a question about divorce by endorsing the passage in Genesis 2.24 which affirms the 'one flesh' of husband and wife, who by their union form a new unit separate from that of their respective families. In so doing Jesus pointed out that in creating men and women God purposed to unite them together within marriage. It seems to me that Paul's condemnation of homosexuality must be seen not only as an endorsement of Old Testament law but also in the light of his view of human sexuality which was derived from the teaching of Jesus. Furthermore Paul had a strong view of natural law, as was common among Jews educated in the Hellenistic world.

It is often said that Paul's view, in the light of the entirely different cultural situation of the world in which he lived, cannot be applied without modification to the situations of our Western world today. It is never easy to make judgments across the centuries from one culture to another; but in the light of what I have said about Paul's views on human sexuality and on the natural law, I have no reason to think that had he lived today he would have radically altered his mind about the principle of homosexuality. In any case many Christians today would not see the need of such sophisticated reasoning about the scriptures. The Bible condemns the practice of homosexuality, and the authority of scripture for them is such that the matter is settled.

Paul used an argument from natural law. It is important to define the sense in which we use that phrase. It cannot mean that the condemnation of homosexual practice is part of universal morality; for it plainly is not. For example, it was approved by many people in ancient Greek and Roman culture. Nor can it mean that homosexuality is elsewhere unknown in nature, for it has been observed in subhuman species.

In this context the natural law should be understood in the light of God's purposes disclosed in the evolution of species. In the world of nature, sexual and asexual reproduction exist alongside each other. Sexual reproduction has the advantage that new characteristics can be introduced into the phenotype by chromosomes contributed by both parents. Sex evolved for the procreation (and survival) of species. But at the emergence of *homo sapiens*, with his ability to form close personal relationships, sexuality took on a new and equally important meaning, expressing mutual love and enhancing the unity between the two persons concerned, and enriching them in their personal being. These are the two aspects of sex in human relationships, and Christians see the emergence of the second from the first as part of divine providence in the process of evolution. For human beings, love is primary. Procreation is a reflection of divine creation: but without human love which mirrors divine love and which is expressed in sexual intercourse, there would be nothing distinctively human about the sexual act.

Human sexual relationships must in principle be open to both unitive and procreative functions. This is not to say that each and every act of intercourse must be open to life; but in principle they need to be. Homosexual relationships are clearly not open to procreation. They involve the use of parts of the body for purposes very different from those for which they evolved. They therefore constitute a denial of the natural law in this respect because, in the words of the Roman Catholic Declaration, they 'lack an essential and indispensable finality', although they do not lack this finality so far as the unitive function of sex is concerned. In the words of the Vatican Declaration, there are 'intrinsically disordered'.

Christians commonly see tradition as one of their sources of authority. Here, until the twentieth century, tradition has been unanimous within mainstream Christianity in condemning homosexual relations. The early Christian Fathers were far more vehement in their condemnation than St Paul. In the mediaeval period it was similarly regarded, and St Thomas Aquinas taught that it was contrary to the natural order. The Reformers took an even more condemnatory attitude. It is fair to say that until the twentieth century no distinction was made between orientation and practice, and homosexuality was condemned throughout Christendom. Christians who take seriously arguments from natural law as well as from scripture, and who pay respect to Christian tradition, are bound to conclude that, objectively speaking, the practice of homosexuality is wrong according to the criteria of moral theology.

Homosexual orientation is, however, quite another matter. If people are born homosexual, their condition is in no way their own fault. Indeed, this is how God made them. They cannot alter their condition: many homosexuals have fervently wished to do so, but have been unable to change. It is a very painful awakening for such people to realize that, in this intimate and personal area of life, they are different from other people. For many years I worked as a Dean in a Cambridge college, and I shall never forget the pain and distress when young men of eighteen or nineteen would come to me, from time to time, to confide in me this newly discovered secret of their personal life. Such a person had reluctantly come to the conclusion that girls had no attraction for him, but on the contrary he found himself drawn not only by friendship but also by sexual attraction to those of his own sex. Earlier he may have hoped that this was a passing adolescent phase which many young people may experience as they grow into adulthood; but the kind of person whom I am describing had slowly and agonizingly come to the conclusion that for him this was a permanent condition of his nature which no kind of therapy could cure.

How can he possibly tell his parents this truth about himself which he has difficulty in comprehending himself? How on earth will his sisters and brothers react? Whatever will his friends think of him? Sometimes he has difficulty in facing his own future. Suicides have been known from this cause. Those who are heterosexual by nature, as I am myself, need, I think, to have been given the confidence of some such person before they can really have empathy with him; or at the very least a very great effort of imagination is needed before they should speak about such people.

You may notice that my tone has changed from the earlier part of this chapter. There I was concerned with as objective a survey as I could make both of the factors involved in making a judgment about homosexual practice under the recognized canons of moral theology, and also with summarizing the official position on this subject of the various mainstream churches in these islands. Now I have changed to a more personal approach: I am inviting you to try to feel what it must be like gradually to become aware that you have an unalterable homosexual orientation which will be with you for the rest of your life. Moral theology is traditionally concerned with the objective moral assessment of human actions; but I now pass to consider the situation of individual human beings before God in the light of their actual personal situation.

It is necessary for our spiritual well-being, as well as for our psychological health, that we should be able to accept ourselves fully as we are, and to love ourselves as we love our neighbours. Psychologically we all need affirmation as human beings; spiritually we need to know that God loves us and has created us to live to his glory. What is more, it is necessary for us to accept this if we are to believe in the goodness of God.

Does not Christianity teach that every man and woman is made in the image of God? That must mean that there is a fundamental and ineffaceable goodness in every individual. We tarnish this goodness through the corrosive acids of sin; but that is our fault. The way we were born, that is not our fault: that is the gift of God.

Could the gift of life for someone with a homosexual orientation turn out to be no gift at all, but a curse? I know that there was once a form of Calvinism which believed in double predestination: that God, in the words of St Paul, created people who are 'vessels prepared for destruction'. But the Church of Scotland no longer holds its members tied to the words of the Westminster Confession, and such a view of the inherent sinfulness of human nature is rightly abhorrent to us. What then about original sin? I do not want to get involved here in a difficult discussion on a difficult subject; but, in whatever way we interpret the very real fact of original sin, it is a bias which affects our whole person, and it is certainly not to be identified with the permanent homosexual orientation which belongs to some five per cent of our population. It is best, I believe, to think of a homosexual orientation as neither a sin (for there is nothing wrong in it) nor a sickness (for it is not a pathological condition that can be cured) but a handicap (which prevents people from enjoying normal married life). God does not interfere with his evolutionary process, and so people are born with various kinds of handicap which mark them out from the norm. Handicapped people deserve not condemnation but admiration for the way they accept their handicap.

Christians have a particular reason to believe that they have been affirmed by God. We believe that Christ died for all; and in so doing he declared us all righteous, or 'justified' us; and that through faith in Christ and his death, we appropriate this gift of divine forgiveness. God has accepted us all in Christ despite our unacceptability; and through faith in him we are enabled to accept his acceptance.

We have all sinned and fallen short of the glory of God; God accepts and affirms those with a homosexual orientation in exactly the same way as he accepts those with a heterosexual orientation.

His gracious action enables us all to have a proper sense of self-worth. Unless we believe in ourselves as loved and accepted by God, and unless we can affirm ourselves as human beings with an intrinsic dignity and worth, we will not be able to set our will to do God's will. If we think that we suffer from a fundamental corruption, we will lack this sense of self-worth or, worse, we will be filled with self-hatred. This will frustrate us and embitter our lives, and we will be unable to be our true selves. There are those who say that this does not matter, because the Christian life is a life of self-sacrifice; but we must have a self before we can sacrifice it, and self-sacrifice must be a voluntary self-offering, rather than something for which we are not responsible.

It follows from this that we all need to be affirmed as human beings, and particularly those with a homosexual orientation, because they so easily feel that they are a despised minority. In earlier days, before a distinction had been made between homosexual orientation and homosexual practice, this could hardly be done; but today this distinction has been accepted by Protestants and Catholics alike. John Stott, a leading Evangelical, wrote in 1984: 'We may not blame people for what they are.'[10] A few years earlier, the Catholic Social Welfare Commission in England and Wales had published a booklet on the pastoral care of homosexuals in which it was clearly stated:

> Homosexuality (or homophilia) is neither morally good nor bad. Homosexuality, like heterosexuality, is a state or condition. It is morally neutral and the homosexual, like the heterosexual, cannot be held responsible for his tendencies.[11]

In the *Letter to Bishops on the Pastoral Care of Homosexual Persons*, issued by the Sacred Congregation of the Faith, it is said that a homosexual orientation is 'a more or less strong tendency toward an intrinsic moral evil; and thus the inclination itself must be seen as an objective disorder'; a statement hardly likely to encourage such a person! But the letter also includes a statement to the effect that there is a need 'to affirm that person's God-given dignity and worth'.[12] The report of the Commission set up by the Church of

England's Board for Social Responsibility includes this passage about a person with a homosexual orientation which was *not* criticized either by the Board or by the General Synod:

> It is of first importance that he should not condemn himself or be condemned by others because of his homosexual orientation, and this means that he should be enabled to recognize it and be encouraged to believe in the possibility of coming to terms with it and putting it to good use.[13]

Should such a person be encouraged to make friends with members of his own sex? David and Jonathan might be cited in favour, with Jonathan's love for David 'passing the love of women' (II Sam. 1. 26). A booklet from the Catholic Social Welfare Commission stated: 'There can be no opprobrium attached to homophile friendships as such. Friendship is good.'[14] It is generally agreed that it is necessary for the emotional well-being of heterosexuals that they should be able to enjoy the company of members of the other sex; and so it would only seem appropriate that homosexuals should be actively encouraged to meet with and make friends with members of their own sex. There are of course dangers here, just as there are dangers for heterosexuals; but there is often more preoccupation with possible dangers than with the well-being of individual people.

It is true, of course, that acquaintance leads naturally to friendship, and friendship may lead naturally to a closer relationship. And so the next question to be asked (and it is a question to which, so far as I know, there is no official pastoral guidance to those with a homosexual orientation): should such people be encouraged to form close one-to-one relationships, in the same kind of way that heterosexual people do? Or should they be warned against forming any permanent loving relationship with another person of their own sex?

Before answering such a question, someone like myself needs to remind himself of the great blessings received from the 'society, help and comfort' of a heterosexual partner. I also need to remember the need for partnership and intimate friendship that seems to be built into the human race. I need to recall that this is a school for unselfishness as well as a source of strength. I need also to remember that enforced loneliness can bring spiritual isolation and spiritual deterioration. If heterosexuals have discovered, as a basic truth of the human condition, that their interior inadequacies can be helped and their wounds healed through the love and affection of a partner, is there not a strong case for homosexuals to find a permanent loving partner to assist in this process of strengthening and healing?

There are the special circumstances of homosexuals also to be borne in mind. I do not pretend to know the facts of the case, but homosexuals seem more likely than heterosexuals to have casual relationships; and perhaps a higher proportion of them indulge in promiscuous sex. If this be the case, it may be because they are driven to these underground encounters by common prejudice against them; or it may have something to do with the homosexual condition itself; and of course many tragically 'miss the mark' in their sexual conduct for the same reasons as heterosexuals. Whatever be the facts and whatever be the reasons, it would seem to be preferable to have a close and permanent one-to-one relationship rather than to have a succession of *affaires*, or to lead a life of casual or promiscuous sex. Is it not then pastorally appropriate, in the actual situation in which such people find themselves, to encourage them to have a close and personal one-to-one relationship with another person of the same sex?

Of course there will be homosexuals, just as there are heterosexuals, who feel a special call to celibacy. Those who receive this call will abjure any one-to-one relationship. The call itself will come from a sense of service, which may involve conditions where the single life is demanded: this form of service may be that of a call to the religious life, or in the Roman Catholic Church to the ordained priesthood. It will be a voluntarily accepted call to self-sacrifice of what is most dear to most of mankind – the comfort of a partner, a home and children. It may be undertaken as an eschatological sign of God's Kingdom where there is neither marrying nor giving in marriage. However the call to celibacy may be heard, and for whatever reasons it may be accepted, it must always be a voluntary acceptance. It is extremely unlikely that a higher proportion of homosexuals than of heterosexuals receive and voluntarily accept such a call.

What are those homosexuals to do who do not receive this call? Are they to be encouraged to form a close one-to-one relationship with a partner, but not share the same home? Are they to be permitted to touch one another? After all, the scriptures refer to the kiss of peace, and friends customarily touch one another in greeting; and on the continent of Europe it is usual to greet another person in a chaste embrace. If homosexuals have a loving and faithful relationship, are they to be allowed no token of endearment? Or are they to be encouraged to act like heterosexuals in all ways except those that are sometimes called 'genital acts'? Or do we leave it to their informed consciences to decide in what ways they express their mutual affection and love? I must make it clear that I am talking here only of close one-to-one relationships of a loving, faithful and permanent nature.

I think here we should remind ourselves of the meaning of sex within heterosexual marriage. For man and wife, sexual intercourse is at its best body language, personal and intimate, deepening mutual attachment, strengthening the couple's mutual faith and hope and love, and carrying private messages of tenderness, affection and worth which every individual needs for his or her well-being. These can help to heal the wounds which everyone bears from childhood wounds or from the buffetings of life.[15] Homosexuals by their nature are denied the procreative faculties of sex. Are they also to be denied any glimpse of its unitive aspects?

According to the Vatican letter on their pastoral guidance – a viewpoint shared, I think, by most other churches – they are. We read:

> Fundamentally they are called to enact the will of God in their life by joining whatever sufferings and difficulties they experience by reason of their condition to the sacrifice of the Lord's Cross. That Cross, for the believer, is a fruitful sacrifice

since from that death came life and redemption. While any call to carry the cross or to understand a Christian's suffering in this way will predictably be met with bitter ridicule by some, it should be remembered that this is the way to eternal life for *all* who follow Christ.[16]

There will certainly be homosexuals who feel the call of celibacy and who decide on this way of self-sacrifice. But there will be others who can find healing and strengthening only through the experience of a permanent loving partnership of body and soul, similar to but not the same as that of husband and wife. Objectively speaking, this way of life is against the tradition of the church. It is against the tenor of scripture. It is contrary to the natural law of human sexuality in that, while it fulfils its unitive aspect, it is not open in principle to the transmission of life. For these reasons the church has formulated a general rule against all homosexual practice which involves genital acts. And such rules are useful. They guard against sudden temptation in the heat of the moment. They prevent a person giving himself the benefit of the doubt. They make a person inform himself about the reasons for the rule, and to formulate his response.

If two homosexuals, despite this general rule, decide in their particular situation to live together in a loving and permanent relationship of body and soul, they will find themselves in a situation somewhat (but not completely) parallel to those who remarry after divorce. Whatever the objective findings of moral theology and the formal teaching of the churches, they may decide on this way of life, having found in their own experience that, subjectively speaking, it is for them the better of two choices. They may have found that, in their case, a life of enforced celibacy leads to intolerable pressures of loneliness, to bitterness of heart, to the festering of internal psychological wounds, and to a deepening of their sense of inner inadequacy and spiritual frustration, not to mention their difficulties in controlling their sexual drives. If, when faced with this particular choice, they decide, in the internal forum of conscience, that they can live better to the glory of God in a full homosexual partnership, how can they stand under condemnation? Should not such persons not rather receive sympathy and support from those who do not suffer from their particular handicap?

5

Abortion and in vitro *Fertilization*

Hugh Montefiore

Abortion is almost as sensitive a subject as homosexuality. Thousands of people have gathered to demonstrate in London's Hyde Park, to lobby members of Parliament to change the present law; and similar crowds have gathered in Washington, DC. Such demonstrations have tended to foster an equivalent reaction on the part of those who believe that the present laws of abortion should be further relaxed, and that abortion is a matter entirely within the province of a mother to decide. As one who recently made an unsuccessful attempt in the House of Lords to reduce the maximum period for a legal abortion in England and Wales from twenty eight to twenty four weeks' pregnancy (other than when the mother's life is endangered), I am only too aware of the strength of emotion that abortion raises. However, I shall attempt first to give an objective account of the theological and moral issues involved, rather than involve myself in matters concerning the law; and I shall then say something about some of the choices and dilemmas with which a woman may be faced in this matter.

There is much mystery and puzzlement surrounding the beginning of human life. No one knows how the processes of human reproduction evolved, although a great deal is now known about the development and growth of a human embryo and foetus. At conception, fertilization takes place when a male sperm fuses with a woman's ovum. Formed out of twenty three chromosomes each from the father and mother, the resulting zygote is a single cell, unique in its combination of genes, containing within itself all the instructions needed to develop into an adult human being. In that sense, it *is* a human being. It is alive, and biologically quite distinct from its mother in that it is a separate organism, although it is absolutely dependent on its mother for nurture, nutrients and protection. The embryo normally transfers from the woman's fallopian tube to her womb where it implants. It is reckoned that some three-quarters of all human fertilized ova die naturally in the process of development, most of them before implantation in the womb, many of them probably suffering from some inherent defect.

After fourteen days implantation is complete, and individual development of the embryo is about to start. This beginning is marked by what is known as 'the primitive streak', which starts to appear around days 14–15. Out of this develop the neural folds, which in turn develop to form the recognizable antecedent of the spinal cord. Within a few weeks the embryo is recognizably a miniature baby. The cerebral cortex develops during the period twenty-five to forty days after conception, electrical activity in the brain can be identified at about eight weeks, and the brain structure is complete around week 12. 'Quickening' is not in itself a significant moment for the development of the foetus: it marks, rather, the mother's consciousness of its greater mobility in her womb. With the help of modern skills of nursing and modern medical techniques, about half the babies born prematurely at twenty-four weeks survive and flourish. Twenty-eight weeks is the maximum length of pregnancy permitted in England and Wales for legal abortion. Pregnancy carried to full term normally lasts nine months.

Abortion is the expulsion or removal of a foetus from the uterus, deliberately procured and induced. There are various methods of carrying this out, dependent to a large extent on the length of the pregnancy. Some are very unpleasant; all involve the deliberate killing of a foetus. The so-called 'post-coital pill', taken within seventy-two hours of intercourse, prevents implantation of the embryo. In the early stages of pregnancy, dilatation and curettage are used, or more often 'vacuum aspiration', which removes the foetus by suction. In China and France abortion can now be procured at this stage by means of a pill which causes the lining of the uterus, in which the foetus has implanted, to slough off; and the foetus is expelled. (This pill is likely soon to be more generally available.) In later pregnancy the foetus is too large for this method. Surgery may be used, in which the womb is evacuated of the foetus, which may have to be dismembered. More common is the use of prostaglandins which induce labour, the foetus having first been killed by injection. In very late pregnancy abortion may have to be by Caesarean section.

Abortion is now very common. In Great Britain there is about one abortion to five live births. Since legalization, numbers have increased; but no one knows the full tally of abortions before legalization, only those abortions that went wrong.

The Roman Catholic Church forbids all abortion absolutely:

From the moment of conception, the life of every human being is to be respected in an absolute way because man is the only creature on earth that God has 'wished for himself' and the spiritual soul of each man is 'immediately created' by God; his whole being bears the image of the Creator, who is its sole end. God alone is the Lord of life until its end; no one can, in any circumstance, claim for himself the right to destroy directly a human being.[1]

Not all churches would agree, although some individual members of other churches would assent to it. Most Anglican churches, like the Church of Scotland, hold that the criteria for abortion should be serious risk or grave injury to the health, whether physical and mental, of the pregnant woman. Some would add to these grave defect in the developing foetus.

What are the theological and moral grounds for these attitudes by the mainline churches? They concern the right to life, whether this is thought of as the life of a potential human person, or the life

of an actual unborn human person. They concern also the status of
an embryo or foetus, and hence its right to life. Is it to be treated
just like a lump of jelly, in the case of an embryo too small to be seen
by the naked eye? Surely we must rule that out, because in the
normal way it will develop and be born and become a human
person. If it is a potential person, how should it be treated
compared with an actual person? Or is it a human being, complete
with an as yet unformed body and a soul (even though the soul is
unable to exercise its powers of will and rationality until the body
has formed)? If so, the embryo should be treated in the womb from
conception onwards with the same respect as if it were a post-natal
human person.

Before we can answer these questions, we have to decide in what
sense we use the words 'person' and 'human being'. It is useful here
to use the distinctions made by the Church of England's Working
Party which produced the report *Personal Origins*:

> The first takes its point of reference from the *continuity of the
> individual subject*. Through and out of the process of pre-natal
> development there emerges an individual, *one* human being,
> whose history it constitutes. Consider the contrast between the
> newborn baby and the old lady, eighty years later, who has
> grown out of that baby: nevertheless we say that the two are the
> same person. Their identity is not simply a matter of material
> continuity (which holds of course only at the level of organiza-
> tion, for the actual molecules are not the same), nor of a
> continuous memory (which does not stretch back to earliest
> infancy, and may incidentally have been disrupted by psycho-
> logical trauma). We call the two the same, because behind every
> presentation of the individual human phenomenon we are accus-
> tomed to discern a subject, a 'someone' whom we call by name,
> who is the bearer of a particular life history ... This approach
> then traces the individual story back as far as fertilization.[2]

The Working Party described the second viewpoint as follows:

> The second interpretation argues that there are attributes which
> must be possessed by a developing embryo before it can be called

a person. Respect is due to an embryo at all stages, but protection of life in the sense that a post-natal child would have it, is afforded only after some particular threshold during pregnancy ... This second approach is based on the special dignity which is displayed by human nature. To be a human ... is to be the subject of powers of mind and soul which set humankind apart from other forms of life. At the root of these powers is the phenomenon of consciousness, and it is as the *subject of consciousness*, the proponents of this view maintain, that we value the human being most fundamentally ... If we are to draw a morally relevant distinction between human beings and other animals, we seem compelled to define the human in terms of a sort of nature able to exercise rational moral and personal capacities. We need to assert that all members of this species possess such a nature, even where, through some impediment, it cannot be properly exercised in many particular cases.[3]

The proponents of this second viewpoint, with which I identify myself, would recognize that consciousness depends on the development of certain physical states, and so they could not regard an embryo as such as a human being. They would wish to err on the side of caution, and thus they would invest a developing foetus with an increasingly personal nature as the nervous system began to appear, the brain structure commenced to develop, and electrical activity started to take place in the brain.

There are those who attribute so high an authority to Holy Scripture that they believe that a definite answer to these difficult questions can be determined from the scriptures. Stott, for example, looks particularly to Psalm 139.[6] He reads there important truths. Verse 13 shows that God directly creates the human person at conception: 'You created my inmost being: you knit me together in my mother's womb.' Because the author uses the same personal pronoun in the psalm before and after his birth (vv. 1, 2, 3, 13), 'as embryo, baby, youth and adult, he is conscious of being the same person'.

Stott finds corroboration for this view in such passages as the saying in Jeremiah: 'Before I formed you in the womb, I knew you' (Jer.1.5)[4]. Looking to the New Testament, he sees special significance in the account of Elizabeth's meeting her cousin Mary in the hill country when 'her baby leapt in her womb' (Luke 1.41). For him this is proof that John the Baptist, as yet unborn, personally recognized the special calling of Jesus, as yet unborn in the womb of Mary.

But the story of the salutation was merely intended to show that Mary, in bearing her child, was like the Ark of God.[5] The other texts use expressions appropriate to the age when they were written, when little was known about foetal development, and when primary causation was attributed to God where today we attribute secondary causation. The texts were not intended to specify what kind of continuity exists between a foetus and an adult. Much more relevant is Ex. 21. 22f., which prescribe a lesser penalty for causing a miscarriage than the death of a pregnant woman, clearly showing that in ancient Israel a foetus was regarded as of less value than a living person.

We simply cannot be certain when a human person, possessing both body and soul, begins to exist. We have seen that it is not a matter of scriptural revelation, and (for those who accept Roman Catholic authority) it has not been and could not be the subject of an infallible definition.

There are several difficulties attached to the idea that the soul is infused immediately at conception. In the first place fusion of ovum and sperm is a process taking some twenty four hours. Secondly, until it is implanted in the womb, the fertilized ovum is capable of both twinning and combination, but souls surely cannot twin or recombine. If God creates souls at the moment of human conception and if most human embryos die before implantation in the womb, he would create most souls to be parted from their bodies within seventy-two hours, which seems most odd. Fourthly, it is some time after conception that there is any differentiation between what will become the foetus, the placenta and the foetal membranes, and so it is not clear into what at that point the soul would be infused. It is also difficult to see how the soul could be infused into the body until the brain begins to develop through which the soul will operate.

There has been a developing tradition in the church on this matter. St Thomas Aquinas, for example, following Aristotle, held that a human being is not created until the human soul is infused into the body, after forty days in the case of a male and ninety days in the case of a female. In the nineteenth century this became a matter of dispute in the Roman Catholic Church. The Dogma of the Immaculate Conception defined Mary as without original sin from the moment of conception, thereby implying that she also had a soul from then on. In a Declaration on Abortion issued in 1974 the Roman Catholic Congregation for the Faith made it clear that 'the question is a philosophical one'. Since it is possible that in every case the soul is infused at conception, there is always the risk in abortion that a human person is being killed; a risk that must not be taken, so that all abortion has always been prohibited.

Other churches have not worked out their official position in such detail. Many Christians today (among whom I include myself) differ from the absolutist position. They assume a process of development during which the growing foetus, as it develops an increasing complexity of organization, achieves new qualitative levels of existence with 'new stages and expressions of being welling up from within.'[6] If this is the case, it is impossible to give a precise moment when a foetus has a soul.

As a potential human being the foetus is always deserving of respect. In most situations it has a right to life; but not in every case. For example, the mother, as an actual human person, if her life is endangered, must have priority over her foetus, which is a potential human being; and in such a case it is justifiable to terminate its life. Those who hold an absolutist view would often agree on this point. (Under the law of double effect, it would be justifiable to save the mother's life, even if a by-product of this action were to be the death of her foetus.[7])

Are there any other situations where abortion may be justified? Some women have abortions because it is inconvenient for them to have a baby; and this is rightly abhorrent to the Christian conscience. Similarly, the idea of using abortion as a contraceptive is inconsistent with the respect that is due to an actual or potential human person.

Views differ about abortion when a foetus, if it were born alive, would have such physical or mental abnormalities that it would be severely handicapped. Those who regard this as the killing of a human person would naturally regard it as immoral. It is a more difficult decision for those who believe that the foetus is not yet fully a human person. Some types of abnormality cannot be diagnosed early on in the pregnancy. Severe abnormalities usually result in early post-natal death. People handicapped from birth who do survive usually prefer to be alive than dead. But they can impose great strains on an already overburdened family. Many mothers would ask for an early abortion in such cases, but they would be more doubtful at an advanced stage of the pregnancy, because the foetus seems to them more nearly an actual human being.

The so-called 'social clauses' are the cause of 98% of all legal abortions in England and Wales today, where the risk of injury to the physical or mental health of the women or her children is greater than if the pregnancy were terminated. (This is capable of a maximizing interpretation. But it can also be interpreted minimally, since the risk of continuing a pregnancy is statistically greater than the risk of termination; and this minimizing interpretation is usually adopted.)

What are the rights of the foetus compared with the rights of the mother who is anxious for her own welfare and the welfare of her family? Christians differ. Some would say that the foetus has always overriding rights. Others would simply say that a woman in such a situation must decide for herself about abortion. Others, among whom I include myself, would say that the deliberate killing of a potential human being could only be justified when there is a grave risk to mental or physical health. Most Christian people, I think, would agree that it is wrong to kill a foetus at a stage of the pregnancy when it would be likely to be born alive and survive, for by that time it surely has an absolute right to life. This used to be put at twenty-eight weeks; but with modern skills and medical technology more than half the babies born at twenty-four weeks live and survive.

I have spoken so far as objectively as I can. But abortion is a very different matter for the women who are involved. I am a man, and like all men I do not know what it is to bear a child within my body, nor do I know what it is to be faced with the prospect of a severely handicapped baby to care for, when life is already an almost intolerable burden. I think that many women agonize in such a situation before they decide to ask for an abortion because they know that they could not cope with the baby; but they know also that, once it is born, bonding will take place and they will not be able to bring themselves to part with it through adoption or for any other cause. Most women want babies, and they will ask for an abortion only after an agonizing self-appraisal.

I have heard of women who have become pregnant through adultery, and whose husbands have threatened to divorce them if they do not have an abortion. Young girls at school may be threatened with the loss of all family support and educational opportunities. Older women may be frightened at a pregnancy, especially as for them there is a risk of abnormality. Women may be warned by their doctor that their health is at some risk if they have another baby. Single women and others may fear that they do not have the financial and other resources to care for the baby when born.

Those who hold the absolutist position will be against all kinds of abortion, for in their eyes it is akin to murder. But others, who assign to the foetus not an absolute but only a conditional right to life, would say that abortion could only be justified if it can be shown that it would have been better had not the child been born.[8] I include myself among those who hold that such situations will include pregnancies which create a grave threat to the mother's life or health, those in which there is a calculable risk of a seriously deformed or defective child, and children conceived as a result of rape or some other criminal offence.

But at the end of the day the woman concerned is in a better position than others to assess the situation. I cannot myself see that abortion for mere convenience or as a means of contraception could ever be justified. But I do not think that people, least of all men, should withhold support from a woman who, after serious thought and acting with an informed conscience, decides to seek an abortion for one of the reasons I have outlined earlier. Her action may be judged objectively wrong by some experts in moral theology, but if, subjectively speaking, the woman concerned is convinced in the internal forum of her conscience that she has acted lovingly and responsibly in the actual situation in which she finds herself, others are in no position to condemn her.

Despite the large number of abortions today, there are many couples who cannot have children, and who desperately want them. This is a healthy desire, since children form one of the two great 'ends' of marriage, and it is only natural that people should be deeply distressed at their childlessness. (It is said that as many as one couple in ten now fall into this category in the United Kingdom.) Unfortunately, because of abortion, there are few children for adoption, except for those in special categories which may well not be appropriate for the average couple. Medical science and technology has developed ways in which the desire for children may now be granted for hitherto childless couples.

The natural way for a woman to conceive is, of course, through sexual intercourse. But it is also possible for a woman to be artificially inseminated with her husband's sperm (AIH) if he has too low a sperm count, or sperms which are insufficiently mobile for him to procreate a child through normal sexual intercourse. If a woman has trouble with her fallopian tubes, so that an ovum cannot pass down, it is possible under laboratory conditions to fuse her husband's sperm with an ovum extracted from her ovary by a technique known as *in vitro* fertilization (IVF). (Such fertilization usually takes place in a laboratory dish, but a new mechanical method of inserting a sperm into the ovum has recently been achieved.) The fertilized ovum is then inserted in the woman, and the pregnancy continues normally. This method may also be used when her husband's sperm count is too low, or his sperm insufficiently mobile for the technique of AIH to be used. IVF may also be used in rare cases when a woman produces antibodies against her husband's sperm. Since her fertilized ovum contains her own chromosomes, it can implant in her womb in the normal way.

These techniques allow a married couple, desirous of children, to have them, something which could not happen in the natural course of events. We need to consider if there are any theological and moral objections to such practices.

In the first place, both techniques divorce an act of love from the procreation of a child. What God has joined together in nature, medical technology can put asunder. Way back in 1970, with rare prophetic insight, Professor Paul Ramsey, seeing new techniques of human fertilization on the horizon, wrote as follows:

> It was out of his love that God created the entire world of his creatures. The selfsame love which in Ephesians 5 becomes the measure of how husbands should love their wives was, according to the Prologue (of St John's Gospel), with God before all creation . . . We procreate new beings like ourselves in the midst of our love for one another, and in this there is a trace of the original mystery by which God created the world because of his love. God created nothing apart from his love; and without the divine love was not anything made that was made. Neither should there be among men or women . . . any love set out of the context of responsibility for procreation, any begetting apart from the sphere of love.[9]

This is a strong argument for Christians who believe that procreation is itself a mirror of divine creation. However, a married couple unable to have children in the normal way do not abjure sexual intercourse. They do not deliberately set out to tear asunder procreation from the act of love. They may be forced into such action because of the defects with which it has pleased God that they should be born. The husband may be present, and indeed participate, in the act of insemination. What cannot be done through sexual intercourse may be achieved through an occasion of mutual love and affection. The resulting child will be their own, conceived with their own gametes. The question facing such a couple is this: is it better that they should accept their handicaps so that their union remains unfruitful, or should they take steps to enable their union to fulfil God's purpose in marriage for offspring, even though this means that their act of love itself cannot achieve this? I think that, faced with such a choice, most couples would rightly take the option which enables their mutual love to bear fruit in marriage, even if not through sexual intercourse.

There are, however, further aspects of the matter to be considered, this time concerning their relationship to the child. Professor Oliver O'Donovan has written:

> The true character of *procreation* is secured by its belonging to the man-woman relationship. The status of the child as 'begotten not made' is assured by the fact that she is not the primary object of attention in that embrace that gave her her being. In that embrace the primary object of attention to each partner is the other. The I–Thou predominates. The She (or He) which will spring from the I–Thou is always present as possibility, but never as project pure and simple. And precisely for that reason she cannot be demeaned to the status of artefact, a product of will[10]

Those who use artificial contraceptives have already begun to walk a little way down that path. Couples (acting in a spirit of wise stewardship of their resources) may try to plan their families with the help of contraceptives. But even so, they do not always have children as and when they wish. There is a large area of contingency, so that children remain a gift through procreation, and never become a product through technology. Of course AIH does not always produce a child, but it is a step further down that road. A couple must decide for themselves whether the use of AIH will demean their child to the status of artefact. The child is to be conceived within the mother's body, nurtured in her womb, and lovingly cared for by parents who actively longed that their union should be fruitful. They must decide for themselves whether this will ensure that the child is looked on as a person in her own right rather than an artefact produced by medical technology. My judgment is that such parents will love such a child and treat her with all respect. If they are themselves convinced that this is so, they are perfectly justified in using this technique.

The position is rather different when the woman's ovum is fertilized with the husband's sperm through IVF. Instead of conception taking place through a personal encounter of a man and a woman, the woman's ovum is impersonally fused with her husband's sperm in a dish, overseen by a white-coated official in a laboratory. The question arises whether a person will be demeaned by knowing that he or she originated in this way. Faced with the alternative possibility that they would not have existed at all, most people would opt for life. Furthermore, if such a child has been nurtured in the mother's womb, and cared for with love and affection by both parents, the resulting mutual affection and bonding between them is likely to predominate over any feelings of unsatisfactory origins. Once again, a couple, if both partners are convinced that this will be the case, is justified in going ahead with this method.

There is a further difference between IVF and AIH. The minor operations involved in extracting and inserting an ovum carry a slight degree of risk. The woman may have only one ripe ovum removed from her ovary; but often more than one is taken, for this improves the likelihood of one implanting itself in her womb. In this case, there is always the chance of a multiple birth, but the woman will know the risks and willingly accept them.

Situations will arise in which it is impossible or inadvisable for one or other of the partners to a marriage to contribute to the begetting of a child. The husband may be infertile, or he may be in danger of transmitting a serious handicap. In that case, his wife may be inseminated by sperm from an anonymous donor (DI, or Donor Insemination). This practice has been current for over forty years, and in Britain alone some 1,500 to 2,000 children are born every year with this origin. There is no law to control the practice, although British law does now insist that children born in this way should be regarded as children of the marriage. It is usual in Britain for a donor to produce sperm for no more than ten children, to reduce the danger of unwitting incest. He is usually paid a small fee and expenses. He remains anonymous to the recipients of his sperm, although known to the doctor administering it, who only acts with the agreement of the husband and who may try to match sperm so that a child has certain of the husband's physical characteristics (e.g. the same blood group).

DI has been compared both with adoption and with adultery. In fact it is like neither.

An adopted child has been conceived by normal sexual intercourse; a child from DI has not. An adopted child may have been dearly loved by its natural parents: it has only been adopted because they were not in a position to rear the child in an appropriate way. By contrast, the only contribution by the biological father of a child by DI is the production of sperm by masturbation, for which he is paid a small fee. An adopted child, when he comes of age, may now (in British law) know details of his origin. A child by DI may not. The most such children may be told when they grow up (and they have no legal right as yet to such knowledge) is the category of person to whom their biological father belonged.

A child born through adultery exists through an act of infidelity on the part of one partner to a marriage, unknown at the time to the other, and is possibly never known to be the child resulting from the act of adultery. A child by DI is not the outcome of marital unfaithfulness. On the contrary, it is a child desired by both partners of the marriage.

Here we may ask two questions. In the first place, to what extent may a child suffer through ignorance of his or her origins, and in particular through ignorance about his or her biological father? This already happens to some children, whether of a prostitute or of a promiscuous mother, who literally may not know the identity of the father. On the other hand, in the case of DI, the child is wanted and loved, and carried in its mother's womb, and surrounded by the affection of its parents, who may very sensibly regard this as the decisive factor. But not necessarily. Only last week someone in his forties, whom I have known for a very long time, told me that he was now embarking on a search for his origins, made difficult by the destruction of documents in the Second World War. He had waited many years until his adoptive mother had died before doing this. It could be the same with someone born from DI.

Is it integral to a marriage that both partners should contribute biologically to their child? Without that contribution, their children cannot be the physical outcome of their love. There are nonetheless certain biblical precedents for having children in childless situations. When Sarah was barren, Abraham took to wife Hagar. This was at Sarah's suggestion, who said, 'it may be that I shall obtain children by her' (Gen. 16.2). Similarly Rachel persuaded Jacob to have a child by her slave Bilhah. Rachel identified herself with Bilhah, saying, 'She shall bear upon my knees, that I may also have children through her' (Gen 30. 3). In a very different situation, according to the Jewish law, when a man dies childless, his brother has the duty of taking her to wife, and raising up seed for his dead brother (Deut. 25.5). These Old Testament precedents are not decisive, but they do seem to show that in certain difficult situations there is a certain degree of openness to unusual remedies. If both partners to a marriage for good reasons strongly desire a child and conscientiously believe that it is right for them to proceed in this way, they should not be condemned. With DI anonymity is preserved by doctors for the security of the marriage and for the sake of the child, but I sometimes wonder whether it might be better to follow the Old Testament precedent of a personal donation of sperm from someone who is known to share some of the husband's genes, preferably from the brother of the infertile husband.

Ovum donation is similar to sperm donation, except that a woman makes a donation in place of the wife, in contrast to a man donating sperm in place of the husband. An ovum may be donated when a wife cannot produce ova, or is likely to transmit a disabling inherited condition, or has a disorder which prevents egg recovery. When an egg is donated in this way, fertilization takes place *in vitro*. The donor's egg implants itself within the body of the physiological mother and is carried by her to full term, and the resultant baby is nurtured and cared for by her and by her husband. All this makes it unlikely that the child when he grows up will feel deprived of his genetic or biological mother; but it is one step further along the road from natural conception resulting from an act of love. Once again, a couple must make their own responsible decision about whether it is right for them to take this path, after they have thought out the arguments for and against; and this decision should be respected.

Embryo donation is another step down that road. It takes place when both husband and wife are unable to produce gametes, so that one donor provides sperm, and another donor provides an ovum, and the egg is fertilized *in vitro* and inserted in the body of the wife who bears the child in the normal way. In such a case both biological parents are anonymous, and the physiological mother who bears the child, together with her husband, constitute the social parents who care for and love the child. The bearing of the child by the physiological mother enables bonding to take place. Perhaps for this reason this technique has been called 'prenatal adoption'; falsely, however, as I have already shown.

If a couple both find that they are infertile, and they badly want a child of their marriage, are they morally justified in asking for embryo donation? Once one starts down this path, exactly where should one draw the line? I myself find it very difficult to see how a child which has no genetic inheritance from either of his or her parents can properly be called a child of the marriage. The child would have no knowledge at all of his or her origins. It would seem to me that in this situation, such a couple should accept the fact of their childlessness. But I have not been in that situation myself, and so I could not pass judgment on a couple who feel so strongly that a childless marriage is maimed and contrary to the purposes of God that they opt for this medical technique, despite the disadvantages and difficulties that I have mentioned.

A further problem arises in this connection. It is customary to fertilize more embryos than are needed to resolve the problems of fertility, so that only the 'best' ones are inserted. Other 'spare' embryos may be frozen and kept for subsequent insertion. Others may be destroyed or used for research. This raises questions about the status of the embryo which we considered earlier in this chapter in connection with abortion. Those who stress the continuity of the human person from the moment of conception will regard this as immoral. For them an embryo should be produced for one purpose and one purpose only, for development within the womb and growth into an adult. Others will wish to respect an embryo because of its human potentiality. They would wish, therefore, that the law should lay down, so far as human embryos are concerned, strict rules about all human interference with the course of nature. At the same time they would not regard the destruction of embryos, or their freezing for subsequent use, as breaching in principle any theological or moral principle, if this were done to assist the relief of childlessness. Similarly, research on human embryos could be welcomed, providing this were done under strict licence, for the relief of childlessness or the alleviation of disease or the elimination of genetic defects, even though consent on the part of the embryo is manifestly impossible. But such research would have to take place within fourteen days of fertilization, when the embryo is still fluid and unformed, and before the 'primitive streak' appears which heralds the differentiation of the blastocyst from its placenta and fibres.

I must also mention surrogacy, when a fertilized ovum from a husband and wife is inserted into the body of a second woman, who bears the child and who at birth hands it over to the natural parents. This may take place because the woman can produce an ovum, but is unable or unwilling to bear a child. To claim that the child belongs to its genetic mother rather than its physiological mother flies in the face of the natural bonding which takes place between a woman and her child when she carries it in her womb. Commercial surrogacy involves a contract, and in Britain this is a crime under the Surrogacy Arrangements Act 1985. There are overwhelming moral reasons against it, in addition to those concerning IVF and embryo donation already considered. A woman is demeaned by womb-leasing, a child is demeaned as being the product of a financial contract, and the bonding between the baby and its physiological mother broken. However, an informal surrogacy arrangement, say between a married woman and her married sister, is not illegal. I find it very hard to justify it myself, but since I have not been in that situation myself, and I do not know the pressures of childlessness or the effect of this kind of surrogacy on the persons involved, I must myself keep an open mind about it.

As for the mainstream churches, the Roman Catholic Church has ruled against all these techniques. The Church of Scotland in 1985 accepted AIH and IVF, but rejected DI, egg-donation and surrogacy and non-therapeutic embryo experimentation. The Church of England rejected surrogacy and embryo donation, but was divided about the other techniques, rejecting them by a narrow majority of its General Synod in 1984; but the following year it reversed its verdict by an equally narrow majority.

These new medical techniques raise questions about the nature of marriage and the status of the foetus before the birth of a baby. I have tried to deal with these. They also raise further questions about which I will make a few final observations.

A healthy desire to have children, when frustrated, may grow into a pathological obsession for a child. This tragic condition must be distinguished from a compulsive desire to have a child for one's own satisfaction and pleasure. Just as some people want to possess consumer goods, others yearn to possess a child, and are prepared to use any method of child production when normal procreation fails. A person is not morally entitled to use these modern medical techniques with such a motivation.

Secondly, a distinction must be made between what is the marital norm and what are special cases of childlessness. We can only contemplate these special techniques for assisted procreation and child-bearing in special cases providing that it is fully recognized that, in the overwhelming number of cases, there is, in principle, no sundering of the act of procreation from the act of love. Exceptions, to be justifiable, must be parasitic upon the norm, or we would indeed be using our new-found techniques to overthrow the God-given ordering of human marriage.

Lastly, these questions raise questions of the dominion of man over the created world. This dominion is God-given, and is therefore to be welcomed and used; but, because humankind is made in the image of God, it must always be exercised in a fully responsible fashion. Men and women have an inherent dignity, and we may only deploy our knowledge and skills to assist them to further the intentions of the Creator.

Each individual is unique and is in the image of God, and therefore techniques such as cloning, or possible miscegenation with other species, are to be abhorred. Because contingency is written into the procreative process, sex determination is likewise contrary to the providential ordering of the transmission of life. Fortunately a detailed examination of these matters lies outside the scope of these chapters.

Abortion and new methods of human fertilization raise difficult problems, involving for their resolution both principles of moral theology and the exercise of the individual conscience. They can only be properly understood within the context of marriage, that 'holy estate' ordained by God where two people are attracted to each other, and share their lives in mutual love and respect, in which their union is blessed with children, and where they themselves deepen their faith and love and hope as they live together as a family, reflecting the family of God. We can only contemplate the use of these techniques if they strengthen the family as God intends it to be.

Notes

1. Introduction to Sexual Ethics

1. J. Mahoney, *The Making of Moral Theology*, Oxford University Press 1987, p. 28.

2. Vatican II, *Gaudium et Spes*, 52.

3. *Gaudium et Spes*, 52.

4. Mahoney, *The Making of Moral Theology*, p. 328.

2. Masturbation and Premarital Sexual Intercourse

1. J.T. Noonan, *Contraception*, Mentor-Omega, New York 1965.

2. P. Buckley (ed.), *Essential Papers in Object Relations*, New York University Press 1986.

3. Paul VI, Encyclical *Humanae Vitae*, 1968.

4. J. Dominian, *Sexual Integrity*, Darton, Longman and Todd 1987.

3. Marriage and Marital Breakdown

1. J. Dominian, *Marriage, Faith and Love*, Darton, Longman and Todd 1981.

2. T. Parsons and R.F. Bales, *Family: Socialization and Interaction Process*, Routledge and Kegan Paul 1956.

3. M. Young and P. Willmott, *The Symmetrical Family: A Study of Work and Leisure in the London Region*, Routledge and Kegan Paul 1973.

4. Vatican II, *Pastoral Constitution on the Church in the Modern World*, 'Fostering the Nobility of Marriage and the Family', 48.

5. *Marriage, Divorce and the Church*, SPCK 1971.

6. *Marriage and the Church's Task*, Church Information Office 1978.

7. R. Chester (ed.), *Divorce in Europe*, Martijnus Nijhoff, Leiden 1977.

8. J. Haskey, *Current Prospects for the Proportion of Marriages Ending in Divorce*, Population Trends 55, Her Majesty's Stationery Office, London 1989.

9. Oliver J.W. Bjorksten (ed.), *New Clinical Concepts in Marital Therapy*, American Psychiatric Press, Washington DC 1985.

10. R.E. Emery, *Marriage, Divorce and Children's Adjustment*, Sage Press 1988.

11. *The Code of Canon Law*, Collins 1983.

12. P. Mansfield and J. Collard, *The Beginning of the Rest of Your Life?*, Macmillan, London 1988.

4. Homosexuality

1. *Sexual Ethics. A Declaration on Certain Questions by the Sacred Congregation of the Faith*, Catholic Truth Society, n.d., para. 8.

2. ibid.

3. *Letter to the Bishops of the Catholic Church on the Pastoral Care of Homosexual Persons*, Catholic Truth Society, n.d., para. 3.

4. *Homosexual Relationships. A Contribution to Discussion*, Church Information Office 1979, para. 168.

5. *Report of the Proceedings of General Synod*, Vol. 12 no. 1, p. 415.

6. Cf. Peter Coleman, *Christian Attitudes to Homosexuality*, SPCK 1980, pp. 205–15.

7. J.S. Spong, *Living in Sin*, Harper and Row 1988 and Marshall, Morgan and Scott 1989, p. 154.

8. *Sexual Ethics*, para 8.

9. Cf. D. Sherwin Bailey, *Homosexuality and the Western Christian Tradition*, Longmans 1955, pp. 1–8.

10. J. Stott, *Issues Facing Christians Today*, Marshall, Morgan and Scott 1984, p. 303.

11. *Introduction to the Pastoral Care of Homosexual People*, Catholic Information Service, n.d., p. 7.

12. *Letter to the Bishops*, para. 13.

13. *Homosexual Relationships*, para. 166.

14. *Introduction to the Pastoral Care of Homosexual People*, p. 7.

15. Cf. J. Dominian, *Sexual Integrity*, Darton, Longman and Todd 1988, pp. 92ff.

16. *Letter to the Bishops* (n.3), para. 12.

5. Abortion and in vitro *Fertilization*

1. Congregation for the Doctrine of the Faith, *Respect for Human Life in its Origin and the Dignity of Creation*, para. 1.

2. *Personal Origins*, The Report of the Working Party of the Board for Social Responsibility of the Church of England, Church Information Office 1983, p. 28.

3. Ibid., p. 29.

4. John Stott, *Issues Facing Christians Today*, Marshall, Morgan and Scott 1984, pp. 386f.

5. Cf. R. Laurentin, *Structure et Théologie de Luc 1–2*, Gabalda 1957, 64–90.

6. Cf. J. Mahoney, *Bioethics and Belief*, Sheed and Ward 1984, p. 21.

7. *Abortion and the Right to Live*, A Statement by the Catholic Archbishops of Great Britain, Catholic Truth Society 1980, para. 22.

8. Cf. *Abortion – An Ethical Discussion*, Church Information Office 1965, p. 27.

9. Paul Ramsey, *Fabricated Man*, Yale University Press 1970, pp. 37f.

10. Oliver O' Donovan, *Begotten or Made?*, Oxford University Press 1984, p. 17.